THE ANGLICAN SYNTHESIS

THE ANGLICAN SYNTHESIS

ESSAYS BY CATHOLICS AND EVANGELICALS

ROGER BECKWITH
W. R. F. BROWNING
BENEDICT GREEN
R. P. C. HANSON
MICHAEL HENNELL
J. L. HOULDEN
E. AMAND DE MENDIETA
LESLIE MINHINNICK
JOHN R. W. STOTT

EDITED BY W. R. F. BROWNING

PETER SMITH
Derby
1964

Peter Smith (Publishers) Limited
24 Saint James's Chambers
Saint James's Street
Derby

FIRST PUBLISHED DECEMBER 1964

© *Peter Smith (Publishers) Ltd.*

PRINTED IN GREAT BRITAIN
in 11pt. Garamond type
BY THE FAITH PRESS LTD
LEIGHTON BUZZARD

CONTENTS

ACKNOWLEDGEMENTS

The editor is very grateful to the authors and publishers who have given permission for extracts from their books to be incorporated in these essays:

Bishop Stephen Neill, *The Interpretation of the New Testament*
(Oxford University Press);

R. C. K. Ensor, *England 1870–1914*
(Clarendon Press);

Prof. H. A. Hodges, *Anglicanism and Orthodoxy*
(S.C.M. Press);

Prof. C. F. D. Moule, *The Birth of the New Testament*
(A. & C. Black);

Canon C. H. E. Smyth, *Church and Nation*
(Hodder and Stoughton).

NO PALE COMPROMISE

by

W. R. F. BROWNING

NO PALE COMPROMISE

ELOQUENT tributes have occasionally been paid to the Anglican Communion as being the Church of Reconciliation, when Anglicans have assured each other that the co-existence of Catholic and of Protestant elements in their Church is no diplomatic compromise or a balanced middle road, but is a genuine unity in Christ of these two historical traditions. The time is appropriate to re-examine this claim. In the first place, the relationship of Catholicism to Protestantism has been explored in a much more sympathetic way by Roman Catholic and Protestant scholars on the continent: what has the Anglican experience to contribute to this debate? Secondly, active adherents of certain schools of thought within the Church of England are manifestly still very much conscious of themselves as being against certain others, and the report issued in 1963 outlining a plan of reunion between the Church of England and the Methodist Church, though signed by all twelve Anglican representatives, nevertheless provoked some vigorous dissent from a section of 'Anglo-Catholics' and a large number of 'Conservative Evangelicals,' who both resisted the proposals, though on different grounds. The contention of this introductory essay nevertheless is that The Anglican Synthesis [1] is a theologically viable proposition and that it is as such that Anglicanism has for some time to come a valid, if humble, rôle to play in the furtherance of the Gospel. The essays which follow will then enable the reader to make his own judgment on whether or not this argument can be substantiated.

The variety of belief and liturgical practice in the Church of England is well known, and some continental Roman Catholics have even spoken of two Churches, 'the High Church' and 'the Low Church.' As evidence of the 'Catholic' side of Anglicanism, observers might point to our use of the creeds and sacraments, our insistence on episcopal ordination, and the provision of a calendar and of a liturgy which bears a clear relationship to the Latin Mass which it superseded, not to mention our architectural and legal heritages from the Middle Ages. The mild [2] Calvinism of the Thirty-nine Articles, on the other hand, clearly represents the other side; so do the leading place assigned to Holy Scripture, and the emphasis in the Ordinal on the ministry of the word; so also the simplicity and absence of ceremonial in many church buildings.

Anglicans of one or the other school have often resisted others' claims to be identical with authentic Anglicanism, and mutual exclusiveness was paraded with deplorable bitterness in, for example, the last years of the nineteenth century.[3] Some of the ablest bishops, like Mandell Creighton, whose aim was simply to administer the law as it stood without admitting any new life or ideas, were worn out by these controversies. We can hardly be surprised that theologians who admire the Church of England and who write of it with affection [4] are yet obliged to characterize its ecclesiological situation as unsatisfactory. There have however existed Anglicans who were not exclusively High or Evangelical and who desired to hold both together—though admittedly they have not been numerous. Thus, it was because of the repugnance of some of the Tractarians for what was best in Protestantism that F. D. Maurice was offended, and though he was no less of the Catholic revival than they were, he never joined the *party*. In this century, Dr. O. C. Quick described the aim of his *Catholic and Protestant Elements in Christianity* (1924) as being 'to elicit and to define some of the different values for which Catholicism and Protestantism have stood, to set them first in opposition and antithesis to one another, and then to suggest that reconciliation is both a need and a possibility.' At his enthronement at Canterbury in 1945, Archbishop William Temple maintained in his sermon that the Church of England 'endeavours to hold together in a due proportion truths which, though essential to the fulness of the Gospel of Christ, are, through the frailty of man's spirit not easily combined. . . . The stresses within the Church, so far as they are due to tensions between divine truths imperfectly integrated by men, are signs of truthfulness and of health. They may easily enough be allowed to cause a confusion of voices. But it is the conviction and the justification of this Church of England that Christ means us to essay this difficult comprehension, to hold together within our Communion of the Catholic Church what may not be put asunder without grievous injury, and to present, as far as we may, the wholeness of the Gospel of Christ.' Three years later Dr. A. R. Vidler wrote in an essay (subsequently reprinted in *Essays in Liberality*): 'Anglican theology is true to its genius when it is seeking to reconcile opposed systems, rejecting them as

4

exclusive systems, but showing that the principle for which each stands has its place within the total orbit of Christian truth, and in the long run is secure only within that orbit or . . . when it is held in tension with other apparently opposed, but really complementary, principles.'

It may be desirable to give here a brief sketch of the beliefs and the fortunes of Catholics and Protestants within the Church of England. There has never been a period in the history of the Church since the Elizabethan Settlement when the Church of England has lacked these schools of thought. 'With one eye upon Catholic squires in Lancashire and the other upon Puritan merchants in London and East Anglia, the Queen and her advisers tried to maintain sufficient continuity of structure to satisfy the Catholics, and sufficient reformation to satisfy the Calvinists.' [5] By the end of Elizabeth's reign episcopacy was established as a necessary part of the Church's structure, and Hooker's conception of Catholicity, with its appeal to scripture, tradition and natural law, had defeated those who desired to frame a Reformed Church that should be entirely regulated by scriptural precedents only.[6] The Catholic divines who returned from exile in 1660 were naturally anti-Puritan, and some six hundred small changes were incorporated in the Prayer Book of 1662. Against both Puritans and Roman Catholics, the Anglican divines of this period appealed to the writings of the Christian Fathers. Their work has been called 'the opening of patristic antiquity,' and 'a signal enlargement of the intellectual horizon of the English Church and the admission of a new stock of facts.' [7] But as perhaps seventy per cent of the parochial clergy had been previously exercising their ministry under the Commonwealth, it is likely that their conformity to the restored Church of England was lukewarm, and that at heart they were Presbyterians or Independents in spite of accepting episcopal ordination. (Clergymen ordained by presbyteries under the Commonwealth were to be ordained by their bishops before St. Bartholomew's Day, 1662, on pain of extrusion.) The High Church divine, John Bramhall, aware of this, is in the Anglican tradition of comprehension when in his *Schism Guarded* he denies that the Church of England should 'excommunicate all material heretics, who follow the dictate of their conscience in inferior questions which are not essentials of faith.' But in the churches of

5

Christopher Wren, so perfectly fitted for the Anglican liturgy, and by means of copes and cushions and bowings to the altar, the Caroline divines emphasized their Catholic heritage and repudiated the apparent contempt for what God had created which seemed to them implied by the Puritan objection to ceremonial actions, liturgical rites and reverence; the idea that matter is evil was common in the ancient world and it was absolutely excluded by the New Testament. Puritans and Presbyterians went out from the Church of England and became Dissenters. But many Protestants conformed, and enjoyed the privileges of Establishment.

The defection of the Non-Jurors in 1689 weakened 'Catholic' influence in the Church of England, which became 'for several decades a prey to the rising tide of rationalism and deism,' [8] and the era which Bishop Tillotson (died 1694) founded was noted for its ethical preaching rather than for religious devotion. 'An application to any study, that tends neither directly nor indirectly to make us better men and better citizens, is, at best, but a specious and ingenious form of idleness' was a typical expression from Tillotson's pulpit. Certainly, the Church was still not without its High Churchmen, among whom were the young Wesleys; by contrast with the non-sacramental temper of the eighteenth century, which was fostered by the Test Act of 1673 (no one could be promoted to any public office unless he declared that in the Holy Communion there is only the substance of bread and wine—it was repealed in 1829), these were diligent about regularly receiving Holy Communion. John Wesley is no doubt more often associated with the Evangelical revival, but there is much in his thought and in that of his brother Charles that is Catholic rather than Protestant. However, after the Evangelical movement had started in Yorkshire and in Cornwall, it was certainly strengthened by Methodism, or rather it made possible the rapid spread of Methodism after 1738. [9] Wesley however held theological views which were not those of the moderate Calvinists of the Church of England, and there was tension between the two groups; the final divergence came in a disagreement about Church Order. Evangelicals within the Church, often banded together in groups, preached justification and repentance and social duties and tried to convert the heterogeneous mixture of both godly and time-serving people who all equally belonged to the English Establishment into something nearer to congregations of faithful men. They met strong opposition, as from Herbert Marsh, Bishop of Peterborough (1819–1839), who had studied theology in Germany and lectured on historical criticism at Cambridge: he propounded a series of eighty-seven questions as 'a trap to catch Calvinists,' and any unsatisfactory answers disqualified such a clergyman from holding a benefice in his diocese.

The Oxford Movement in the nineteenth century reasserted the English Church's claim to be one with the Catholic Church of the ages. For some, this meant judging the present in the light of the early, undivided Church—as with Father Benson of Cowley. Others adopted devotional and ceremonial practices of the Counter-Reformation.[10] Either way, it emphasized that the Church is a visible society, the divinely instituted means of salvation, held together not only by the inward action of the Holy Spirit, but also externally by the episcopate in the apostolical succession. A doctrine of the Eucharistic Sacrifice and Real Presence was taught without any inhibitions, and Catholic vestments increasingly crept in.

The early celebration of Communion every Sunday morning had been already introduced by Evangelicals, such as Daniel Wilson at Islington, and Anglo-Catholics followed suit. Moreover they invested the Eucharist (which was sometimes a High Mass without communicants) with outward splendour. Unfortunately the ceremonial customs and the doctrinal emphases of Anglo-Catholics led to untold bitterness and strife, and their use in small parishes upon the arbitrary fiat of a new incumbent was often responsible for something like a local dechristianization. But since the nineteen-thirties Catholic Anglicans have been increasingly influenced by the ideals of the Liturgical Movement, which is opposed to clericalism and religious individualism and is wide open to ecumenical encounter, and by biblical scholarship, both Protestant and continental Catholic. Sir Edwyn Hoskyns, who addressed the Anglo-Catholic Congress in 1930, also translated Karl Barth's *Epistle to the Romans* and preached a notable course of sermons on the Thirty-nine Articles in the chapel of Corpus Christi College, Cambridge.[11]

As an exponent of 'Biblical Theology,' which emphasized the themes of God's Judgment and God's mercy, and which spoke vividly to the inter-war generation, Hoskyns undoubtedly drew Catholics and some Evangelicals together. Both alike welcomed the principle that basically the New Testament witness is a unity and that it is unique and distinct from the religions and culture that surrounded it in the Jewish and Gentile worlds.[12]

What Hoskyns opposed was theological Liberalism. By this is meant not that he ignored modern thought or the methods of biblical criticism, though he was suspected of doing so. He felt rather that biblical criticism itself destroyed the Liberal portrait of Jesus. 'Like many other Cambridge scholars, Hoskyns gave some of his time to the correction of the examination papers of boys and girls . . . ; as he read the answers to the New Testament papers, he was horrified to discover the extent to which the whole religious teaching in schools had come to be dominated by a liberal presentation—a Bible from which the supernatural had been carefully excluded, a calmly rational presentation of the miracles, a Jesus of Nazareth who was admirable as teacher and example, but from whom all messianic and divine attributes had been pared away.' [13] The theological Liberalism which Hoskyns attacked for its shallowness took too optimistic a view of the human situation, and great New Testament words like redemption and resurrection were given a different content.[14] Thus, sin was merely the disagreeable survival of animal traits that man had inherited in the course of evolution from lower species. (There *have* been Anglicans who have taught this, though such radical Liberalism is not found among the 'permissible' opinions outlined in the report *Doctrine in the Church of England* (1938) which certainly included those which represented ' the high tide of liberal theology in the Church of England.') [15] Theological Liberalism, however, in the sense of the grateful use of human reason, has always been dear to Anglicans (witness the Cambridge Platonists) and has influenced most of them—in varying degrees. It was the determination to be open to biblical criticism that obliged Charles Gore to modify the traditional doctrine of the inspiration of scripture when he wrote his contribution to *Lux Mundi* (1889) and which enabled the Christian faith to remain tenable for many educated people. In it 'one breathes again that air of larger freedom which frightened Newman into the prison-house of absolutism' (P. E. More).

8

Through *Lux Mundi* the powerful solvent of biblical criticism gradually penetrated the Church of England, and, at a not inconsiderable cost of suffering, blazed a trail whose principles have in the end been quietly taken over by others, and are now common property except in extremely Conservative circles. Liberal principles have influenced both Anglo Catholics and Evangelicals, but the fact that Catholics did not isolate the authority of the Bible from that of the Spirit-filled Church from which the Bible emerged, certainly made them less anxious to repudiate notions of doctrinal development or pseudonymous authorship than Evangelicals, who have been deeply divided, as will be evident from essays in this book. There have also been Anglican Liberals (as there have been Catholics and Evangelicals) whose primary loyalty has been to their school of thought or party organization rather than to the Church of England as such; their existence was assured by the Gorham Judgment of 1850, which was a declaration by the Privy Council that a clergyman could not be required to relinquish his office if he denied the doctrine of baptismal regeneration.[16] Liberal, or Broad, Churchmen were delighted by the acquittal before the same secular court ten years later of five of the contributors to *Essays and Reviews:* it seemed that the State was determined to ensure the maximum of liberty within the Church—but with the consequence that Catholics began to be contemptuous of authority altogether so that gradually, but widely, the adaptation or reinterpretation of Anglican formularies became almost part of the Anglo-Catholic way of life.

In Anglicanism then we have these two main types of Christian faith. It may be useful to summarize some of the distinctive qualities of each, as a prelude to the later essays of this book.

The Catholic doctrine of justification is that this is the gracious work of God, which is completed when God accepts sinful man who has, by grace, been sanctified and become worthy of being accepted. Catholicism will not have God's justice compromised by allowing any fictitious righteousness. The Protestant doctrine emphasizes that God justifies the sinner as he is, without conditions. Then whereas the Catholic speaks of Christ *in* the Church, the Protestant emphasizes Christ's Lordship *over* the Church; so that for the Catholic the visible Church, with a hierarchical structure, is necessary for salvation, while the Protestant

9

emphasizes that each individual needs to make a personal response to God; and when the Church's ministers are ordained, this act of Christ does not confer a capacity to do what other Christians are unable to do, but sets aside certain people to act representatively on behalf of Christ and of the whole Christian body. The sacraments for the Catholic are the means by which we are brought into the life of Christ and the sermon expounds how this living in Christ can be worked out from day to day, whereas the Protestant tends to think first of the Bible and preaching as how the Lord gives himself to men, and the sacraments may become optional public demonstrations to seal what has already been received. Liberal Anglicans continue to make sure that neither Catholics nor Evangelicals are deaf to scientific and historical studies, or to the new knowledge that must be assimilated in Christian ethics. Yet it must be admitted that human sin has sharpened the difference between these main types, and as they confront each other with an armoury of statements and legal opinions and trusts, each to exclude the other, it requires an immense effort not only of intellectual insight but also of repentance and humiliation to progress towards unity.

It is in some respects a welter of liturgical variety, unco-ordinated strategy and doctrinal arrogance. The Church of England could seem to be no more than an uneasy compromise held together by the machinery of the Establishment. Meanwhile, on the continent, Roman Catholic and Protestant theologians are discussing differences with a new frankness and a new appreciation of the positive affirmations of the other system. It was in 1954 that Father Louis Bouyer published his *Du Protestantism à l'Eglise* (English translation, *The Spirit and Forms of Protestantism*, 1956), which at once attracted attention for its interesting suggestion that properly understood the principles of the Reformation were valid and would have recovered authentic elements of Catholicism had they not been vitiated by negative aspects which Bouyer associates with nominalism, i.e. 'what was most corrupt in Catholic thought at the end of the Middle Ages.' It is true that this book was marked by a certain asperity towards Protestants, but as the dialogue has developed, this discordant note has been silenced. Father Geiselmann says that 'the new understanding of Holy Scripture, dawning simultaneously on Catholics and Protestants alike, has torn down the walls which separated them for centuries.' In the same book (*Christianity Divided*, 1961), Dr. Hans Küng examines the doctrines of justification and sanctification; and 'the biblical categories must be the standard against which they are checked.' It is said by one of the editors of *Christianity Divided*,[17] that Dr. Küng had elsewhere established that the full Catholic doctrine of justification did but explicitly affirm all that was nearest to the hearts of the Reformers.[18] Among Protestants, Dr. Oscar Cullmann's labours of rapprochement are well-known.

But the Church of England is much more than a practical compromise, and we venture to claim that its *raison d'être* is the existence within its communion of both main strands of western Christianity. The Anglican Synthesis is the affirmation of a paradoxical unity, a prophetic intuition that Catholicism and Protestantism, though in the past they have encased the Gospel in mutually antagonistic systems, are not ultimately irreconcilable. Are they perhaps complementary to each other, as in the Bible creation and revelation are correlative manifestations of the same reality? After all, in the New Testament different writers are concerned with one or with the other—St. Paul, in 2 Cor. 5 : 17 etc., being primarily concerned with creation and new creation, while St. John prefers to speak of a New Birth in which God is known, and of sin as a refusal to receive Light (John 15 : 22). Sometimes indeed the difference of emphasis and expression in the New Testament has been pushed much wider than this, as by B. H. Streeter,[19] who found seven main types of theology (i.e., there is no such thing as '*a* New Testament theology') but even if this is exaggerated, there is indeed a variety of legitimate positions in the New Testament. There were, for example, the Jewish Christians who believed it vital for Christians to observe the whole Law of Moses, and there were also the followers of St. Paul who passionately denied this : yet this disagreement was not allowed to divide the Church at the Lord's Table.

'E. Käsemann has pointed out that Christian theology, in some of its early phases, represents a conflict between opposing schools, all alike appealing to the authority of the Spirit, but in very different ways—"enthusiasm" (in the technical sense of that word) with miracle-working (reflected perhaps derogatorily in Matt. 7 : 22–5), a Jewish and rabbinical type of organization (note

B

Matt. 23: 8–10), legalistic Judaism (for which some might quote Matt. 5: 17–20, though it can be otherwise interpreted), and, at the opposite extreme, the kind of liberalism and universalism for which perhaps Stephen stood. Different outlooks, embodying different structures of society, criss-cross confusingly in the dim background of the New Testament, within Jewish Christianity as well as in Gentile Churches. In the last analysis, a good deal of it can be expressed in terms of varying eschatologies. Some groups perhaps saw the conversion of the Jews as the first necessity before any further spread of the Gospel; others, led by St. Paul, looked for the reverse process: only when the full complement of the Gentiles had come in would all Israel be saved (Rom. 11:25).' [20] And while some demanded human effort, others expected an intervention from God.

The variety of theological expression in the New Testament does divide into two main types. Dr. F. J. Leenhardt actually traces them to Abraham on the one hand, who set off on a new venture at God's word, which is the source of the Protestant type, and to Moses on the other, in whose life God uses places and institutions as the means of giving himself to his people, and this is the Catholic way. With the spirituality of Abraham we should presumably associate a dynamic idea of God, prophecy, justification by faith, personal holiness: with Moses, a metaphysical idea of God, the Church, the Law, sacrifices, sacraments and liturgy. And if these two types of faith are complementary because both are found in the Bible, then both should be held together in one Church. It may be that those Churches that have opted for clarity and precision by excluding one strand of Christian tradition are less true to the complexity of the Bible than Anglicanism which, from historical necessity, has embraced both. We might say therefore that Catholicism and Evangelicalism are necessary to the fullness of the Church in this present age, just as vocations to marriage and celibacy are also complementary to each other. (For if some were not called to celibacy, marriage would not be a vocation at all, but merely the biological norm. Nevertheless it is only a temporal vocation; at the End what is merely complementary and insufficient will disappear, Matt. 22: 30.) Catholic Anglicans and Evangelical Anglicans are in full communion; we use the same liturgy in the 1662 or one of its revised forms; Anglicans kneel together to receive the Lord and his power; clergy and laity are in constant conversation in deaneries and dioceses and Congresses; there could be a continuous process of mutual influence, and there is no inquisition or board of deputies to prevent an Anglo-Catholic from introducing extempore prayer, or an Evangelical from advocating auricular confession. Indeed this is the sort of thing that is known to happen—but too rarely—as indeed it happened in the past with great parish priests—like James Adderley, who said of a former vicar of St. Alphege's, Southwark, 'From dear Father Gouldon I learned to combine the best in Evangelical religion and the best in Catholicism—or, rather to know that, rightly understood, it is that they are not two religions but one.' [21] It may be that this was eclectic stuff, lacking theological depth, though there was certainly no lack of dedication or heroism in those old 'Catholic Evangelicals.' At the present time Anglo-Catholics are inclined to discard customs that had been borrowed from mediaeval and Post-Reformation Roman Catholicism; there is a new assessment of episcopacy and the concept of apostolical succession, taking account of its apparent vagaries in the course of history and of unacceptable consequences (e.g. the status of the *episcopi vagantes*) of the doctrine in its old formulations; much ecumenical honey is being gathered into the Catholic hive. Evangelicals, though more deeply divided than ever before into Liberals and Conservatives, are open to the possibilities of liturgical revision,[22] as Catholics are too. The prospect of a union between the Church of England and the Methodist Church carries with it the hope that Anglicans will the better grow in personal holiness and that the Anglican Synthesis will be not weakened, as some have suggested,[23] by a preponderance of one type of spirituality, but strengthened by Methodism's sacramental devotion (inherited from the High Church side of the Wesleys) and evangelical fervour and qualities of corporate life which are more like those of Russian Orthodoxy than to any other Christian tradition. This to many Anglicans is an attractive, if as yet elusive, vision.

If there is any validity in the idea of the Anglican Synthesis, what are we then to say of those who have disputed the claim of the other side to be faithful Anglicans? Perhaps out of principles that have been erected into prejudices and then interpreted with the political arts of deception and expedience, God is making a Church where all these have been used to prevent us from slipping contentedly into one type or the other of Christian faith. No doubt F. D. Maurice had good reason to be suspicious of parties in the Church. 'He was convinced that the process of organizing people in defence of particular sets of Church principles results in distorting the proportion of the faith, in admitting a spirit of propaganda which is very different from a zeal for truth, in substituting a Pelagian idea of unity in our possession of certain opinions for the right idea of unity in our common reception of the gifts of God.' [24] At the same time, if ritualists in the nineteenth century had not flouted authority and flamboyantly laid claim to the Catholic past, the Anglican Communion could have become just one of the smaller Protestant sects, with no special ecumenical function. And perhaps it is the providential rôle of Conservative Evangelicals at the present time to put question marks against too easily accepted fashions, and against the contemporary inclination, from which even the Liturgical Movement is not exempt, to regard the Christian faith as no more than commitment to an altruistic way of life, and to remind us, uncomfortably, that our Anglican Synthesis is not after all the magic formula for the *final* unity of all separated Christians.

If any practical programme follows from all this, it might be as follows:

1. Mutual toleration of Evangelicals and Catholics is essential, and the kind of litigation which continued until as recently as 1945 ought not to be resumed.

2. Peaceful co-existence however—the usual condition today, except for occasional outbursts in Parliament when Church affairs are discussed—is not sufficient. Each must explicitly affirm what is valuable in the other tradition without denying the validity of its own. Both have a share in the Anglican past, and historical evidence should not be presented selectively.

3. This should lead on in the future to new theological and liturgical expressions, to more adventurous and costly pastoral experiments, and a new urgency towards Reunion at large.

4. But the ultimate synthesis will not be the work of flesh and blood, but must await the Lord's revelation at the End. As the New Testament itself shows, human language is incompetent to systematize completely the fluidity and complexity of human thoughts and the paradoxes of experience.

In the conviction that some of this programme could be attempted two conferences of Evangelical and Catholic clergymen belonging to the diocese of Blackburn were arranged at Whalley Abbey in 1962 and 1964. We were fortunate in having the Bishop of Southwell (the Right Reverend Gordon Savage) to speak first and to initiate the dialogue, and although what happened was on a smaller scale than the Catholic-Evangelical Congress envisaged by Father Geoffrey Curtis [25] it was not without significance.

It is a selection of papers read at these conferences that comprise this volume, with the exception that the Rev. L. Minhinnick has written his contribution especially for this symposium, and it takes the place of a paper on the Church which was delivered by another theologian without a manuscript and which was unfortunately not therefore available afterwards for publication. It was not part of our scheme to have more than one paper on the same topic (except that there were two papers from different standpoints dealing with the Bible), but four of the contributors belong to the Catholic School and four to the Evangelical, though we were assuming that the Catholic tradition of the Church of England is something bigger and wider than Tractarianism and its successors; two of the Evangelical contributors (Mr. Stott and Mr. Beckwith) are *Conservative* Evangelicals; Mr. Minhinnick and Mr. Hennell are not. None of the contributors would necessarily accept all the opinions expressed in this introduction.

NOTES

[1] Synthesis is here taken to mean not a merging of two or more traditions to form one organic whole, but the acceptance of two or more traditions as necessary to each other within the one organism. But cf. p. 155.

[2] i.e. by contrast with the Calvinist Westminster Confession which was drafted in 1646 in place of the articles.

[3] And in 1922 the Doctrinal Commission 'was appointed because the tensions between different schools of thought in the Church of England were imperilling its unity and impairing its effectiveness,' as the chairman (Archbishop William Temple) wrote in his introduction to the *Report* (1938).

[4] Like Père Congar (cf. his memoirs, *Informations catholiques internationales*, I. vi. 64).

[5] Owen Chadwick in *From Uniformity to Unity 1662–1962* (1962).

[6] J. S. Marshall, *Hooker and the Anglican Tradition* (1963).

[7] Mark Pattison in *Isaac Casaubon* (1875), quoted by A. R. Richardson, *History Sacred and Profane* (1964). Not that the Carolines adopted identical positions: thus in exile some (e.g. John Cosin) communicated with the Protestants, while others (e.g. George Morley) did not.

[8] P. E. More in *Anglicanism* (1935), p. xix.

⁹ See, e.g., C. A. Buchanan in *Anglican-Methodist Relations: Some Institutional Factors* (1961), p. 43.

¹⁰ Evidence in the Report of the Royal Commission on Ecclesiastical Discipline (1906).

¹¹ See Archdeacon Cobbam's article in the *Church Quarterly Review* for July–September, 1958, which contains long extracts from these sermons.

¹² More recent examples of Catholic and Evangelical approximation are their understanding of the corporate nature of the Church (as in the late Fr. L. S. Thornton's *Common Life in the Body of Christ*, 3rd ed., 1964, and Dr. F. W. Dillistone's *The Structure of the Divine Society*, 1951) and the contribution of both to the Anglican Liturgical Movement through 'Parish and People.'

¹³ S. Neill, *The Interpretation of the New Testament, 1861–1961* (1964), p. 214.

¹⁴ Cf. R. Gregor Smith: 'Liberalism may be described as the effort to extract from the teachings of the Bible certain timeless and eternal truths which may be suitably applied to every human situation, e.g. belief in the inevitable progress of mankind,' *The New Man*, 1956, p. 78.

¹⁵ A. R. Vidler, *The Church in an Age of Revolution* (1961), p. 200. See the Report itself, p. 61.

¹⁶ Gorham was himself a Calvinist, but it was Broad Churchmen who gained from the State's determination to keep the Church comprehensive despite what bishops might prefer.

¹⁷ p. 307.

¹⁸ But the Italian Protestant V. Subilia, with perhaps more theological realism, denies that the 'semi-Pelagian phrases' of Trent can be coaxed into Lutheran orthodoxy. What about a Mariology which implies creaturely co-operation in the process of salvation? (*The Problem of Catholicism*, 1964, p. 41).

¹⁹ In the *Cambridge Ancient History* (xi), The Rise of Christianity.

²⁰ C. F. D. Moule, in *The Birth of the New Testament* (1962), p. 172.

²¹ Dieter Voll, *Catholic Evangelicalism* (1963), p..87.

²² L. E. H. Stephens-Hodge, 'Prayer Book Revision: An Evangelical View,' *Church Quarterly Review*, July 1964.

²³ e.g. Mgr. H. F. Davis in *Faith and Unity*, September 1963, on the *Report of Anglican-Methodist Conversations:* 'The main result of a reunion would be to strengthen the Evangelical wing of the Church of England. . . . Anglicans can only hope to unite with Methodists on the lines of their evangelical theology.'

²⁴ A. M. Ramsey, in *F. D. Maurice and the Conflicts of Modern Theology* (1951), p. 38.

²⁵ In *Mirfield Essays in Christian Belief* (1962), p. 209.

THE AUTHORITY OF THE BIBLE

by

R. P. C. HANSON

THE AUTHORITY OF THE BIBLE

A T one point during the coronation of Queen Elizabeth II, the Moderator of the Church of Scotland handed the Queen a Bible, with the remark, 'These are the lively oracles of God.' This phrase, which comes from the sixteenth century, reflects accurately the opinion of the Bible which had been almost universal up to that century. The Bible had been treated as a collection of oracles. So oracular was it regarded that people used to consult it on any problem which was troubling them by opening it at random and taking to apply to their predicament whatever verse their finger happened to stop at. Similarly the gang of former pirates, when they want to black-ball one of their nefarious crew, in R. L. Stevenson's *Treasure Island,* cut out a piece of a printed Bible and used it as their 'Black Spot'; so numinous, so oracular, so magic was the Bible thought to be. To the early Christians the obscurer parts of the Old Testament certainly *looked* oracular, especially the Psalms and the prophets. They had behind them a tradition of oracular treatment of the Old Testament in ancient Judaism. The literature of the Qumran Covenanters revealed in the Dead Sea Scrolls, for instance, betrays this. The author of the *Habakkuk Commentary,* to take only one instance, regards the utterances of the first two chapters of the book of Habakkuk as so many isolated predictions couched in mysterious language but all referring to the events of the commentator's own day, and fulfilled in them. The early Christians read their Old Testament in what was, by modern standards, a bad Greek translation, the Septuagint. Many points of Christian edification and devotion had their origin in a mistranslation. For instance, from the second century onwards many people (first among them Justin Martyr) believed that somewhere in the Psalms the statement was made that the Lord would reign *from a tree,* and this conviction resulted in some fine pieces of devout fancy, not least among them the hymn of Venantius Fortunatus, which is still widely sung:

> 'Fulfilled is all that David told
> In true prophetic song of old.
> Amidst the nations, God, said he,
> Shall reign and triumph from a tree.'

19

In fact there is no statement in the Hebrew text of the Old Testament (nor indeed in the Septuagint) that God would reign from a tree. The mistake may have arisen from some Greek translator attempting a translation of the word 'Selah,' after some such phrase as 'The Lord reigneth.' He did not know what 'Selah' meant, and so he put down a Greek word which sounded like it—*xylou* (from or of a tree). So the mischief was done. The Hebrew text itself presents some examples of a similar process, when the last line of Psalm 87 runs 'All my fresh springs are in thee,' words which have no connection at all with what has gone before. This sentence is no doubt the name of the tune to which the Psalm was to be sung in the service of the Temple, and from the margin or the foot-note it has crept into the text. We could well imagine a similar mistake happening to one of our hymns in, say, three thousand years' time. The hymn is printed as to be sung to 'The Londonderry Air,' but in three thousand years' time no one will have ever heard of the Londonderry air, and so eventually this title will find its way into the hymn itself in some such form as this:

> We praise Thee, Lord, that Thou hast blessed
> Thy people gathered here.
> May we in heaven with Thee enjoy
> The Londonderry air.

This is the sort of thing that happens if any text is treated as oracular. Corruptions and interpolations become canonized and finally sacrosanct.

But we today know, or ought to know, that the Bible is not a collection of oracles, but a collection of ancient documents of varying date in many ways like other such collections. The Bible in its different styles, vocabularies, and ways of handling its subject is like other documents of the same periods and types. Our great, great grandfathers used to refer to the Greek of the New Testament as 'the language of the Holy Ghost,' because it was like no other sort of Greek which they, trained as they were on Classical literature, had ever met, and they assumed that the Holy Spirit had chosen a special sort of language to impart a special sort of message. We can no longer use that description of it because archaeology has now turned up in the sands of Egypt many documents using the sort of language which is to be found in the New Testament, and it has proved to be, not the special language of the Holy Spirit but the language of the lower and middle classes in the Roman Empire, the language of traders, farmers, and soldiers. We can divide the literature in the Bible into many different forms—history, saga, law, hymns, poetry, etc. There are very few oracles among them. When St. Paul was writing his letters he did not think that he was writing oracles, neither did St. Mark when he was writing his Gospel. Even that literary form which has the greatest appearance of being oracular and obscure, the apocalypse, has many parallels in ancient Jewish literature. These documents also have the limitations of their period. Their geography is ancient geography. They witness to a belief in a flat earth. The earth is for them the centre of the universe. They belong to a long pre-scientific age in their conceptions of anthropology, human anatomy, medicine and physics. These documents make several mistakes in history. The thirty-first verse of the fifth chapter of the book of Daniel, for instance, in its description of the circumstances of the accession of Darius I to the throne of the Persian Empire is totally irreconcilable with established historical facts. The speech attributed to Gamaliel in the fifth chapter of the book of Acts places the rebellion of Theudas before the rebellion of Judas, whereas Theudas' revolt took place at least thirty-eight years after that of Judas, and indeed some years after the date at which Gamaliel is supposed to be speaking. No: the Bible is not a collection of oracles. It is even doubtful whether anything is gained by calling it 'inspired.' [1]

What then *is* remarkable about this collection of books? They have, of course, some very fine passages of literature in them. The fortieth chapter of Isaiah ('Comfort ye, comfort ye, my people,' the Gospel according to St. Handel), the twenty-third Psalm, the utterances of Amos ('Let judgment roll down as waters and righteousness as a mighty stream'), and the hymn of love in 1 Cor. 13 are among them. But that is not enough. Other ancient documents have fine passages—the plays of Aeschylus, the speech of Pericles over the Athenian dead in Thucydides' history. Anyway, the Bible does not consist wholly of fine passages. Most of it, in fact, does not strike an impartial reader as impressive from a literary or aesthetic point of view. The books of Judges, of

Leviticus, the Gospel of Mark and the Epistle of James, for instance, are pedestrian in style and unimpressive in manner. Much of the Bible is not in any sense inspiring. Who, for instance, could be inspired by the verse 'a pomegranate and a knop, a pomegranate and a knop, in the border thereof round about,' which occurs in the book of Numbers? And in what sense can this verse be described as inspired? So it is not satisfactory to commend the Bible as inspiring literature.

Neither will it do to commend the Bible as a sort of divine cross-word puzzle, as is done by that wearisome list of fanatics and lunatics, the Jehovah's Witnesses, the British Israelites, the Christadelphians, *et hoc genus omne.* The conviction that the Bible contains minutely detailed predictions which are being fulfilled in the reader's own day is a type of—I will not call it exegesis—a type of neurosis which has afflicted Christians from a very early period. A Syrian bishop about the year 200 led a large following into the desert to await the end of the world in accordance with biblical prophecy. When the world failed to co-operate with his calculations, he got into trouble with the local Roman governor who thought he was starting a rebellion. Similar delusive fixations appear among the minority movement in the Franciscans in the thirteenth century, among many groups at the Reformation, among a number of simpletons who in the last century identified Louis Napoleon with the Beast from the abyss, and a hundred other examples of similar exegetical intoxication could be adduced from past history and from our own day. History has inexorably proved them all wrong. Why should their contemporary imitators be right?

The single unique point about the Bible is its *subject.* This, and this alone, is what gives the Bible its grandeur, its perennial attraction, and its claim on us. What is that subject? The brotherhood of man? The necessity of loving others? The importance of magnanimity and humanity? Equality? Kindness to animals? Pacifism? Tolerance? No. You will find very little mention of most of these subjects in the greater part of the Bible, virtually none, for instance, in Judges, in the books containing the Law, in the books of Kings, in the Revelation./The Bible's subject is the activity of God in redeeming men, God's activity towards mankind carried out in that peculiar manner in which he chose to offer us access, friendship with himself, life with himself. He chooses his people and he sends his Son; we read of the acts, and finally the supreme Act of God towards men. All other subjects are either subordinate to this or not mentioned at all in the Bible. The Bible has been finely called The Book of the Acts of God. We could call this subject, put differently, the disclosure of himself by God to man. This is the Bible's subject, and this is what makes the Bible unique. No other book treats the subject in this way, for no other book could do so.

But why could no other book do this? We can answer this question in answering another. In what form does the Bible convey this subject to us? Not as mysterious oracles, not as inspiring pieces of literature, not as a series of elaborate cross-words. The form of the biblical record is *witness or evidence*. The Old Testament is the deliberately-preserved witness to God's activity towards the Jewish people: witness to the significance of man as God's creature (Genesis); witness to the character and activity of God in the history of God's people (the historical books and even more the prophets); witness to the total claim of God on man (the law-books); witness to the worship and religious life and religious experience of the people of God (the Wisdom literature). The New Testament is the deliberately-preserved witness to the activity of God in his Son who became a man, who expressed fully and finally God's ultimate Act towards us, when the Word became flesh and dwelt among us. The Bible, then, is not an anthology of oracles nor a source-book of inspiring passages nor a divine *Old Moore's Almanack*, but a collection of evidence—evidence of God's acts.

Now, consider the nature of evidence. We are concerned with the evidence of ancient documents, but I will take a more modern example for illustration, the evidence given at a trial, say the trial of a man for fraud. This evidence varies in kind. It may include documents, conversations, letters, account-books. Some of this evidence is more relevant, some less. The accountant's report on the man's books is very likely to be put in as evidence, but so may a sketch of his relations with his wife at the relevant times. This evidence may be inconsistent in details; his defending counsel will produce evidence that the man is careful, conscientious and honest, the prosecutor that he is careless, extravagant and dishonest. This evidence can involve many apparently quite unimportant matters, for instance, what time the accused's secretary leaves the office, or the hotels that he stayed in during a holiday on the Riviera when he unaccountably had money to spend. The evidence need not be inerrant nor infallible nor even complete. What matters is the general effect or drift or weight or impression of the evidence. On this the jury or the judge make up their minds.

All these conditions apply to the Bible considered as witness or evidence. The evidence varies widely in kind. It embraces myth, legend, saga, law, history, hymnody, proverbs, the lives and the utterances of seers, love-songs, philosophical works, parables, apocalyptic, biography, letters, Gospels, sermons, theological treatises. The dates of these vary from 1200 B.C. to A.D. 100, and they are presented in three different languages. Some of the Bible's evidence is barely relevant—Song of Solomon, Esther, 2 Peter. Some of it is intensely relevant—Deuteronomy, Isaiah, Psalms, Gospels, Paul's Epistles, Acts. The Bible is a stained-glass window with a light behind it; it has a clear blazing centre with light gradually dimming to the periphery till we reach a region where we cannot be sure that anything at all can be discerned. The Bible's evidence is inconsistent in details without this inconsistency affecting the whole. It would be strange, indeed suspicious, if it were not. It involves many to us unimportant matters—the provision of parapets for houses, David's amours, Nehemiah's self-importance, the man who had a love affair with his step-mother, the self-assertion of Diotrephes, the worship of Zeus at Pergamum, and so on. But the evidence of God's activity is enshrined in these documents and conveyed through them. The Bible is evidence, raw material, not a blue-print for the form of the ministry, nor a manual of ethics, nor a text-book of doctrine. It is not inerrant. What matters is its general drift or effect or impression or meaning. Did God act towards the Jews? Did God act in Christ? These are the questions which it answers.

The Bible, then, is evidence, but it is evidence for the acts of God, and therefore it is different from all other sorts of evidence and witness. It is written from faith to faith, by those who believe for those who believe, by the Church for the Church. Outside the context of a worshipping community the Bible is inevitably misunderstood and distorted. This is what happens when, for instance, 'the ideals of the Sermon on the Mount' are taken as constituting Christianity apart from the life of the Church. The Bible is written for those who believe in God and worship him, not for scientists, anthropologists, historians, psychologists or novelists, not even for theologians. Nevertheless it has a capacity for continually arousing faith in each age. This is not a magic or sacral quality residing in the pages or words, but the power of God to whom it witnesses. The Bible is a perennially contemporary book, not because it is full of modern science, psychology, crime or romance, but because it witnesses to the acts of God, who is contemporary. This is why we need contemporary translations. St. Paul, for instance, did not write the equivalent in Greek or 'Ye needs must be subject, not only for wrath, but also for conscience sake,' but of, 'You ought to submit, not only out of a fear of consequences, but also out of a sense of moral duty.' The Bible provides the basic material for the life, the prayer, the worship, and the behaviour of the Church. That is why it needs to be studied. The Bible is the raw material which the Church interprets, absorbs and adapts, and has always interpreted, absorbed and adapted.

We may therefore draw our argument to a head by saying that the authority of the Bible is the authority of Christ himself, to whom the Bible witnesses; that it is the Church's task to commend and interpret the Bible, and at the same time to submit itself to the Bible as far as is possible. This position of at once interpreting and submitting to the Bible is not an inconsistent one. There is a perfectly good analogy at hand in the judge who at once interprets the law and does his best to submit his judgment to it, and not to control it. In fact, this position of at once interpreting and submitting has been traditionally the position which the Church has occupied towards the Bible ever since the formation of the canon of the New Testament. The Church commends the Bible to us, but we do not believe the Bible on the authority of the Church, though we may read the Bible on the Church's authority. The Church and the Bible are inseparably bound up together. In no conceivable circumstances could any one encounter the Bible, whether in the form of a written or printed book or in a broadcast, or in the form of Christian teaching, without the activity and mediation of the Church. But the Church can do no more than point people to the Bible, because ultimately the

Church's authority is founded upon the institution of Christ, and the Church has no other proof of its institution by Christ than the Bible. One has only to ask the Church, 'Why should I believe you?', and until the Church produces the Bible and says, 'My authority is written here,' the only possible argument is the futile repetition, 'You must believe me because you must believe me.'

The Bible is a living book. It has, of course, some peculiar, almost (but not quite) adventitious advantages. It uses compelling, vivid and universal images: father, shepherd, blood, war, water, city. It uses poetry, as in Isaiah, the Psalms and the Revelation. It describes perennial human situations: the situation of Joseph and his brothers, of Naomi and Ruth, of Ahab and Jezebel and Ahab and Naboth, of David and Bath-Sheba; the Prodigal Son, the Good Samaritan, the Unforgiving Steward. The Bible is part of European culture now. But beneath and through all these it witnesses to the acts of a living God. It records the living Word of a living God. It is the vehicle of a living Spirit, and therefore it is itself alive.

NOTE

[1] Perhaps I should make it clear that I emphatically deny that Mr. Beckwith's account of inspiration is either really biblical or anything but utterly incredible.

THE INSPIRATION OF HOLY SCRIPTURE

by

R. T. BECKWITH

C

THE INSPIRATION OF HOLY SCRIPTURE

THOUGH this essay has a different title from that of the preceding chapter, I must at once make it clear that its subject covers some of the same ground. I have not attempted anything so impossible as to speak about the inspiration of Scripture without speaking about its authority. Professor Hanson's paper and my own are rather two rival accounts of its authority—my own an attempt to determine what authority Scripture has if its inspiration is affirmed, and Professor Hanson's an attempt to determine what authority Scripture has if its inspiration, in what I conceive to be the historic and biblical sense of the word, is denied.

THE HISTORIC FORMULATION OF THE DOCTRINE

In saying this, I am conscious of at once taking up a controversial position. Few theologians, it will be answered, even of the most Liberal, deny the inspiration of Scripture: on the contrary, they affirm it. The difference between Evangelicals and others, it will be added, lies not in the affirmation or denial of inspiration but in the meaning that is given to the word. Of course, in a certain sense this objection is justified, but in a much more important sense it is not. Theological terms, like 'inspiration' or 'resurrection' or 'divinity,' have a long-standing historic meaning, which normally goes back to the teaching if not the very language of Scripture, and it does not help discussion if they are used in a completely new sense. Unfortunately, those who break with traditional Christian teaching on crucial issues have always been very prone to defend themselves against the charge of heresy by continuing to use traditional language. The late Dr. H. D. A. Major, for a long time editor of *The Modern Churchman*, whom many that do not share his views will remember with affection, once wrote that he had never met a Modernist who did not believe in the resurrection and divinity of Christ. But to talk in this way is really just an abuse of language. The survival of the human spirit is not the same thing as resurrection, and the creation of man in the image of God is not the same thing as divinity. Similarly, the concession that Scripture is in some very loose and uncertain manner connected with revelation, is not the same thing as inspira-

29

tion. Whatever points may have been left undetermined in the Church's traditional doctrine of inspiration (as certain points have in every doctrine) it was always until the last century held to mean that Scripture, owing to the activity of the Holy Spirit in its composition, is not only fully human but also fully divine, and therefore wholly true: that Scripture, as our own formularies put it, is 'the very pure word of God' (preface 'Concerning the Service of the Church' in the Prayer Book), that it is 'God's word written' (Article 20), so that no passage of Scripture may be interpreted in such a way as to contradict another (Article 20 again), since otherwise all passages could not be alike true and the whole 'infallible,' as they are affirmed to be in the Homily entitled 'A Fruitful Exhortation to the Reading of Holy Scripture,' in the Homily 'Concerning Prayer,' and much more fully in the Homily entitled 'An Information of them that take offence at certain places of Holy Scripture.'

This is not only the teaching of the Anglican formularies, and of the great classical divines of the Church of England,[1] but it is also the historic teaching of the Christian Church as a whole. It was the teaching of the Reformers—certainly of Calvin (despite the unhistorical attempt by some Barthians to read back their own teaching into his writings) and even of Luther (as more and more modern scholars are maintaining).[2] It was the teaching of the mediaeval Scholastics—witness not only Wyclif, who states that 'Scripture is the infallible and necessary rule of truth' (*De Veritate Sacrae Scripturae,* cap. 24), but Gerson (*De Examine Doctrinarum*), Bonaventura (*Breviloquium*), Thomas Aquinas and others. Aquinas says 'It is unlawful to hold that any false assertion is contained either in the gospel-narrative or in any canonical scripture, or that the writers thereof have told untruths, because faith would be deprived of its certainty, which is based on the authority of Holy Scripture' (*Summa Theologica,* secunda secundae, qu. 110, art. 3. Cf. also *Contra Gentiles,* lib. 4, cap. 29). Going back further still, it was emphatically the teaching of the Fathers. Long catenas of their assertions to this effect have been compiled by Routh (in his *Reliquiae Sacrae*), Lee (in his *Inspiration of Holy Scripture*), Westcott (in his *Introduction to the Study of the Gospels*), Sanday (in his *Inspiration*) and others, and for the sake of brevity we shall omit them here, but simply take note of the mistakes of the late Gabriel Hebert on this matter in his well-known book *Fundamentalism and the Church of God.*

Hebert, like some others before him, thought he could find a different doctrine in Origen (of all writers) and Jerome. Origen's phrase *error scripturae* (the original Greek is not extant) in his comment on Matt. 27: 9 does not mean 'an error of Scripture' but, like *mendum scripturae,* means 'an error of writing.' It probably here refers to a scribal slip, not a mistake of the original author. Jerome, in his 57th Epistle, certainly speaks in rather surprising terms of the manner in which New Testament writers translate passages from the Old, but his point is that they give the general sense instead of troubling to find the equivalent of every word. This does not mean that they are careless, for he says it is his own method also when translating; nor that they make mistakes, for this he explicitly denies. Indeed he goes so far as to affirm that the very order of words in Scripture is a sacred mystery. And if, in one or two passages of the epistle, he speaks as if the New Testament writers have made a mistake of translation, he may simply be drawing the logical conclusion from the principles of his critics. In any case, what he says here must be read in the light of his teaching elsewhere—in his 53rd Epistle, where with reference to Leviticus and Revelation he maintains that under every word of Scripture mysteries lie hid; and in his 82nd Epistle, where he says that the apostles are unlike other writers in that they do not commit errors. There is nothing, therefore, in these passages which is really opposed to the great torrent of assertions from Justin Martyr, Irenaeus, Tertullian, Dionysius and Clement of Alexandria, Origen himself, Julius Africanus, Eusebius, Methodius, Basil, Gregory of Nazianzus, Gregory of Nyssa, Augustine, Gregory the Great and others, who maintain that Scripture neither errs nor deceives, that seeming contradictions cannot be real, and that no syllable is without its importance, since the words of Scripture are the utterances of the Holy Ghost, and it is rash and presumptuous to suppose otherwise. H. P. Liddon, Pusey's great disciple, therefore knew what he was doing when he contended, against Gore, that to surrender biblical infallibility is to surrender not only the authority of Scripture but the authority of catholic tradition as well.[3] For (as Roman Catholics still recognize) there is nothing on which tradition is more unanimous than the infallibility of Scripture.

Personally, being an Evangelical, I would not lay such weight on tradition as Pusey, Liddon and their Anglo-Catholic successors do. But it seems pertinent to point out that those few Anglo-Catholic writers who still maintain the infallibility of Scripture—men like P. J. Thompson,[4] G. B. Bentley [5] and S. C. Clark [6]—are men who realize the logic of their own position in a way which the numerous Liberal Catholics who have followed in the footsteps of Gore apparently fail to do.

Such then is the Church's immemorial doctrine of the inspiration of Scripture, and the curious assertions of Hebert, J. K. S. Reid and other contemporary writers, to the effect that the infallibility of Scripture is a modern theory, are as far as they could possibly be from the truth. The only evidence they can offer is that in the period before the Reformation allegorical exegesis had far greater vogue than it has had since, so that, *in effect,* to assert the infallibility of Scripture was not the same thing before the Reformation as it is today, since it then led on occasion to different consequences. Naturally, the views one holds on interpretation do make a difference to one's theology, but unless we believe that before the Reformation allegorical exegesis had such license that it could make anything mean anything, this does not fundamentally affect the issues of inspiration and infallibility. Actually, before the Reformation tradition controlled exegesis with a pretty firm hand, and the scope that it gave to allegorical exegesis was to supply an additional meaning and not a substitute for the primary meaning. Consequently, it is true and not really at all misleading to say that, whatever other differences there may have been between them, those who preceded and those who followed the Reformation agreed on the infallibility of Scripture.[7]

THE BIBLICAL BASIS OF THE DOCTRINE

It is necessary, however, to push our enquiries still further back. An Evangelical cannot, like the traditionalist, simply assure that the traditional doctrine is taught in the Bible, or at least that nothing contrary to the traditional doctrine is taught there. The ultimate basis of faith for the Evangelical, and his only ultimate basis of faith, is not tradition, nor reason, but Scripture. If the historic doctrine of inspiration is contrary to Scripture, or even absent from Scripture, he cannot regard it as an article of faith.

It is natural to ask why, and the Evangelical has in fact a good answer, in the witness which the Holy Spirit, dwelling in the hearts of Christians, bears to the biblical gospel. Our Lord in the Fourth Gospel repeatedly claims this sort of attestation for his own teaching (John 7:17; 8:43–7; 10:26–30; 18:37), and St. John makes the same claim for *his* teaching (1 John 4: 4–6, cf. 2: 20, 27), as St. Paul does also for *his* (1 Cor. 2: 6–16). But the witness of the Spirit is not simply a doctrine of Scripture—it is a fact of Christian experience, known in some measure at least to every converted Christian. The Evangelical is not, therefore, arguing in a circle, as he is often charged with doing, if he argues the authority and inspiration of Scripture not from the teaching of Scripture as such, but from the teaching of Scripture as attested by the Holy Ghost. Anglo-Catholics are similarly open to the charge of arguing in a circle when they try to prove the final authority of tradition or the Church, and they have, I suggest, no answer to the charge.

What then does the Bible, and more particularly our Lord and his apostles (those for whom the witness of the Spirit is explicitly claimed) say about inspiration? If we are willing to listen to their teaching on any subject at all, we should be willing to listen to their teaching on this subject also. Yet the curious thing is that, in this age of 'Biblical Theology,' we find theologians willing to listen to the Bible on almost every subject except itself. C. H. Dodd's book *The Authority of the Bible*, J. K. S. Reid's book *The Authority of Scripture*, Raymond Abba's book *The Nature and Authority of the Bible*, even Karl Barth's book *The Doctrine of the Word of God*, though their professed subject is the authority of Scripture, give practically no attention, or none at all, to anything the Bible has to say on it.[8] What the reason may be—whether the fear of arguing in a circle, or of having to draw what they call 'Fundamentalist' conclusions—I do not know, but the fact remains. And this in face of the further fact that there exists a voluminous, learned and penetrating literature on the subject from the conservative standpoint, expounding the biblical teaching—a literature which these writers feel themselves entitled to ignore without attempting to answer it, or perhaps even reading it.

Since this literature is so little known outside Evangelical circles, perhaps I may be permitted to mention a few titles. Important work was done on this subject in the sixteenth and seventeenth centuries—indeed, if we look back to Wyclif's *De Veritate Sacrae Scripturae*, earlier still; though little was done before Wyclif's time, because, as with other doctrines, the authority of the Bible did not have treatises devoted to it until it became a topic of controversy, which prior to Wyclif it was not except in apologetics against the heathen. To confine ourselves to relatively recent works, however, and works which may be read in English, so many have been produced in the nineteenth and twentieth centuries that it is somewhat difficult to select. Perhaps the most important are Louis Gaussen's *Theopneustia*, for its systematic and comprehensive character,[9] William Lee's *Inspiration of Holy Scripture*, for its wealth of historical information, and B. B. Warfield's *Inspiration and Authority of the Bible*, for its precision and penetration. Warfield's book is, I believe, still in print in this country, published by Marshall, Morgan and Scott; and so are J. W. Wenham's valuable lecture *Our Lord's View of the Old Testament* and (in a more polemical vein) J. I. Packer's vigorous little treatise *Fundamentalism and the Word of God*, which are published by the Tyndale Press and the Inter-Varsity Fellowship respectively.

Let us turn now to the New Testament teaching. The word 'inspiration' (*theopneustos*, literally 'inspired') occurs once in the New Testament, in 2 Tim. 3: 16. It is used to denote the influence of the breath of God in the origination of the Scriptures, and its implications are drawn out elsewhere in a variety of ways. Thus, according to the New Testament, the Scriptures are 'the oracles of God' (Rom. 3: 2; Heb. 5: 12), spoken 'by the Lord through the prophets' (Matt. 1: 22; Acts 1: 16 etc.); they *must* be fulfilled (Matt. 26: 54; Acts 1: 16 etc.); 'It is written' (literally 'It stands written'), 'Have ye not read?' or 'It is contained in Scripture' puts an end to all controversy (Matt. 4: 4; Mark 12: 10; 1 Peter 2: 6 etc.); 'Scripture says' means 'God says' (cf. Rom. 9: 17; Gal. 3: 8), and 'God says' may be predicated of quotations where God is so far from being the ostensible Speaker that he is referred to in the third person or even addressed (Heb. 1: 7–12); the historical writings share this divine authority (Rom. 4: 3; 1 Cor. 15: 45; Gal. 4: 21; Heb. 7 etc.); and all Scripture is authoritative, down to 'jots' and 'tittles' (Matt. 5: 16–17. Cf. Luke 16: 17), so that arguments can be confidently rested upon a single word or word-inflection (Matt. 22:43-5; John 10:34; Gal. 3:16; Heb. 2:8, 11-12; 3:7-4: 11; 7: 2; 1 Peter 3: 5-6 etc.).

It will be noticed that this is the teaching of our Lord and the apostles, as well as the other New Testament writers. It will be noticed also that it excludes all the variations on the Evangelical view which have been popular since the rise of Liberalism, and have now been taken over by the 'Biblical Theology' movement. Thus, according to the New Testament, not just the writer but also the writing is inspired; there are no degrees of inspiration, for all is alike the word of God; no different kinds of inspiration are recognized; not just the explicitly doctrinal or oracular but also the historical books are inspired; not just the main body of Scripture but also its details are inspired; it is not just partly but wholly the word of God—the word of God itself, and not just the medium through which the word of God comes.

That this is not merely the apparent but also the real meaning of the New Testament teaching is confirmed by the context in which this teaching was originally given. Our Lord and the apostles were first century Jews, and it was to first century Jews that their preaching was in the first instance addressed, whether in Palestine or in the synagogues of the dispersion. First century Jews also formed the nucleus of the congregations to which the epistles were addressed. Now, it is a well-established fact that the Jews of the first century, and indeed of several centuries earlier, believed in the infallibility of Scripture. Thus, in the Apocrypha the Book of the Law is on two occasions virtually identified with the divine Wisdom (Ecclus. 24: 23; Bar. 4: 1), and some words of Moses from Deuteronomy are introduced with the remarkable expression 'As thou spakest by thy servant Moses in the day when thou didst command him to write thy law before the children of Israel' (Bar. 2:28). Among the Pseudepigrapha, the Book of Jubilees speaks of numerous injunctions in the Mosaic Law (Jub. 4: 5; 6: 22; 15: 25; 16: 29-30 etc.) and even of an inference from the narrative of Genesis (Jub. 28: 6) as 'ordained' or 'written' or 'engraved' 'on the heavenly tablets.' In the Dead Sea literature, *God* is said to have spoken, *through* the prophet Isaiah, the words of Is. 24: 17, and is twice said to have spoken through Moses words which, according to the narrative, he simply

35

addressed to the lawgiver (Zadokite Document, col. 4; War of the Sons of Light, col. 10; Hymns, col. 17). The expression 'It is written,' and another New Testament formula, 'God says,' become in these writings customary means of introducing quotations, even from narrative (Manual of Discipline, cols. 5, 8; Zadokite Document, *passim*); and the Book of Joshua is in one place said to be a history which *God* recorded, by the hands of his anointed, the men who had vision of things fore-ordained (War, col. 11). The belief of Philo in the absolute and verbal perfection of the Scriptures is well known, and is evident upon the least acquaintance with his writings. His arguments frequently turn upon a single word. He treats narrative and legislation as equally divine. He not only continues the use of the formula 'God says' to introduce citations, but employs for the purpose many impressive expressions of his own. And his theory concerning the psychology of inspiration, however vulnerable and peculiar, could only have been formed by one who believed in the God-given character of Scripture down to every detail. This brings us to the time of our Lord, but, to complete the evidence from Judaism down to the end of the first century and the close of the apostolic period, Josephus affirms that the canonical books are received as the work of prophets only, who by inspiration learned what they wrote, including historical matters, from God; that therefore the Scriptures are in perfect harmony, nor has any man ever dared to make a change in them.[10] While the rabbis of that century (and indeed of two centuries earlier), if one may trust the entirely consentient evidence of their sayings as written down at a later date in the Mishnah, were in full agreement with the view of Philo and Josephus.

Now, if our Lord and the apostles had wished to teach some different doctrine from that commonly accepted by their hearers, they would have had to make the fact very clear. In reality, what they do is to use language which could only be understood as confirming in its essentials [11] the doctrine which their contemporaries already held. Their very choice of words has close Jewish parallels, some of which we have seen, while others are noted in the relevant parts of Strack-Billerbeck's *Kommentar zum Neuen Testament* and in Oepke's article on *grapho* and its cognates in Kittel's *Woerterbuch*.

36

Actually, it is sometimes admitted by Liberal writers that the New Testament does in fact endorse the Jewish view of inspiration. Thus Brunner, in the appendix on the authority of Scripture in the first volume of his *Dogmatics,* admits that the apostles probably accepted the Jewish doctrine of verbal inspiration. It does not seem to perturb him at all that the doctrine taught in his *Dogmatics* is completely different.

EVASIONS OF THE DOCTRINE

Certain evasions of this teaching—I do not think they deserve any kinder description—have been current in the last hundred years. The first evasion is the kenotic theory (or rather theories) of the incarnation, popularized in this country by Gore, who was attempting to deal with this very issue, and to evade our Lord's teaching on the Old Testament.[12] Kenotic theories have come under such heavy fire lately that I do not propose to deal with them at length. They are in effect a denial of the incarnation—a conversion of the Godhead into flesh, such as the Athanasian Creed warns us against—and I suppose most of those present, if Evangelicals, would incline more to G. C. Berkouwer's presentation of Christology, or if Anglo-Catholics to E. L. Mascall's.[13] The exegetical basis for the kenotic theories has been utterly exploded,[14] and those, like Vincent Taylor,[15] who still maintain a sort of kenoticism, do it in spite of rather than because of the biblical evidence. One further difficulty of these theories may be mentioned —that they prove too much. Kenoticists wish to say that our Lord, despite his mission as 'teacher' and 'prophet,' despite the fact that he was the incarnate 'Word' and 'Wisdom' and 'Truth' of God, was unreliable in some of his teaching. They do not wish to say that he was unreliable in all of it. He was unreliable in historical, scientific and critical matters, not however in religious matters.[16] But the authority of the Old Testament was for our Lord a profoundly religious matter of great importance. If he was unreliable on this, he was unreliable on religious matters also, and no bounds at all can be set to his unreliability.

Another evasion is the theory of accommodation—that our Lord accommodated his teaching to the beliefs of his hearers in order to avoid unnecessary offence. The difficulties of this theory are manifold. First, it is not in accordance with our Lord's practice in other matters—on the related subject of tradition, for example, he outrightly attacked Pharisaic beliefs (Mark 7: 1–23). Secondly, it is difficult to maintain this theory in a meaningful way without attributing to our Lord the immoral practice of encouraging his hearers in their errors. Thirdly, if the theory had been true, we would find our Lord using the Old Testament when it suited his purpose, but not making explicit assertions of its divine authority, as in Matt. 5: 18; John 10: 35, or even implicit ones, as in Matt. 22: 29; Mark 7: 8–9, 13; Luke 16: 29–31, and not using the earnest language in his appeals to it which we find him using (Mark 7: 6 etc.). Fourthly, if the theory had been true, we would presumably find our Lord manifesting a different attitude to the Old Testament when the multitudes were not present. Actually, in his private teaching of the disciples, both before and after the Resurrection, his attitude shows no perceptible difference (Matt. 26:24; Luke 24:25–7, 44–7; John 13:18), and this is confirmed by the fact that the sermons and writings of the disciples, to say nothing of the rest of the New Testament, indicate clearly enough that they had never been taught any other doctrine. Even in the temptation in the wilderness (Matt. 4: 1–11; Luke 4: 1–13) and in prayer to his Father (John 17: 12) our Lord displays the same attitude.

DIFFICULTIES OF THE DOCTRINE

We pass on now from evasions to real difficulties in the doctrine. Like every other true doctrine, the doctrine of inspiration has its difficulties, and they are not few. But in examining these difficulties, we ought to come to them not in the normal modern manner of being ready to surrender inspiration at the first breath of doubt: rather, we ought to come to them with a consciousness of the great presumption, I might even say the invincible presumption, that since the doctrine of inspiration is a doctrine of the gospel, there must be an answer to its difficulties whether we can see the answer or not.

Some of these difficulties arise from our Lord's own teaching, especially in the Sermon on the Mount, and are not very difficult to answer. There are two important facts to notice when approaching the Sermon on the Mount. First, that our Lord pauses at the beginning of it to exclude the kind of misinterpretation which is common today—the idea that it is directed in any way against the teaching of the Old Testament (Matt. 5 : 17–20). Secondly, that the formula used by our Lord in quoting the Jewish teaching on which he here comments is not 'It is written' (viz., in the Old Testament) but 'Ye have heard that it was said to them of old time.' It appears therefore to be oral teaching—Pharisaic tradition [17]—on which our Lord is commenting. Such oral tradition was not, of course, something quite apart from the teaching of the Old Testament, but it at once embodied, interpreted and amplified the latter, as with the words 'hate thine enemy,' quoted and repudiated by our Lord in ch. 5, vv. 43–8.

Approaching the Sermon in the light of these two facts, we note that in the cases of the prohibitions of murder, adultery and forswearing (ch. 5, vv. 21–37), our Lord by no means contradicts these Old Testament principles—rather, he adds to their stringency, in accordance with vv. 20 and 48. In the case of 'an eye for an eye' (ch. 5, vv. 38–42), he appears to be criticizing the extension of what is in the Old Testament a thumb-rule for judges to our private relationships. In the case of divorce (ch. 5, vv. 31–2), he is once more moving in the direction of greater stringency: whereas Moses prohibited divorce without proper formalities and divorce followed by a renewal of the marriage, our Lord, save in the instance he mentions, prohibits it altogether. Matt. 19 : 3–9 is an important comment on this passage, since it shows that our Lord is not appealing to a principle foreign to the Old Testament, but to one embodied in the Book of Genesis. And there is no suggestion that the concession of Moses to Israel's 'hardness of heart' in the period of their spiritual immaturity was without divine sanction, even if only a temporary sanction : for it is easily understandable that not until the fullness of time were they ready for the restoration of marriage to the state in which it had existed before the Fall. A similar approach is called for by our Lord's attitude to the sabbath and unclean meats in other parts of the gospels (Mark 2 : 28; 7 : 18–19). Even if he abrogated (or, to speak more accurately, 'fulfilled') the Mosaic legislation on these subjects, this is very far from meaning that the latter was without divine authority in its own age. Rather, our Lord is claiming, as the One who instituted the Law, to have the right of interpreting, spiritualizing, and in its literal sense abrogating it. And with the sabbath, as with divorce, he is appealing not from the Old Testament but to it (Mark 2 : 25–6; cf. Matt. 12 : 3–5), requiring that the Fourth Commandment be interpreted in the whole context of Scripture.

Another exegetical difficulty is the fact that our Lord is presented in the New Testament as the Word of God (John 1 : 1, 14; 1 John 1 : 1; Rev. 19: 13)—is it not a return to Judaism then, if we treat the Bible as such? Of course, Evangelicals do not treat Christ and the Bible as the Word of God in the same sense. Christ is the Word of God in the highest sense, as being the eternal Son of the eternal Father—as being himself God. But since, outside the period of his ministry, Christ is reliably known only through the spoken or written witness of the prophets who preceded it and the apostles who followed it, there does not seem to be any reason why their witness should not be called the word of God in a secondary sense, as their *spoken* witness is in the Old and New Testaments themselves. This answer will not satisfy everybody. Many will want to ask whether ideas like verbal inspiration and propositional revelation are not too materialistic—whether they do not imply a mechanical process involving dictation, and whether they do not make the Bible the real god of the Evangelical. If these questions are asked by those who worship the sacrament of the altar, it would be easy to reply with a *Tu Quoque*, but such a reply would be unworthy of the seriousness of the questions posed. To deal with these questions then, and first with that of dictation : all reputable Evangelical writers reject the notion that dictation is the normal mode of inspiration,[18] and they do not believe that their conception of inspiration implies it. Scripture is obviously the outcome of a fully human process of composition, being marked by the individuality and initiative of its writers, but such is God's perfect sovereignty in his providential operations, embracing even the voluntary activities of men (Gen. 50 : 20; Prov. 21 : 1; Acts 2 : 23 etc.), that there is nothing to prevent a fully human process of composition being also fully divine. With regard to verbal inspiration, when Evangelicals assert this they are not thinking of words in independence of the sentences and books which they constitute—they are thinking of words as the indispensable media of thought. F. D. Maurice [19] is among those who can be instanced as recognizing that if the *words*

'beget' only of children in the first generation (see Gen. 10: 13–18; Deut. 4: 25; 23: 8, and compare the flexible use of other terms of descent). Passages worth comparing are Ezra 7: 1–5, certainly an incomplete genealogy (cf. 1 Chron. 6: 3–14), and Exod. 6:20, which tells us in a very circumstantial way how Amram's wife, Jochebed, bore him (not his immediate offspring but) his descendants of several centuries later (cf. v. 18; Num. 3: 17–19, 27–8 etc.).

It is not just a possibility, however, that the genealogies of Genesis are selective. There are two facts which make this practically certain. First, the genealogies (in the Septuagint at any rate, which includes the name of Cainan at ch. 11, vv. 12–13) are strikingly symmetrical: they have the same number of generations as each other, and the same number of names in each generation. This strongly suggests that they have been deliberately made symmetrical (like the genealogies of Matthew 1) by the omission of unimportant names. Secondly, the statement in Gen. 10: 25 that the earth was divided in the days of Peleg is a significant one. For unless names have been omitted from the genealogy in the following chapter, Noah, Shem, Arpachshad, Shelah and Eber were also alive at the time. These two facts make it highly probable that the genealogies are selective, and so allow the period which they cover to be many times multiplied. At this point the problem merges into that of creation and the appearance upon the earth of what the Bible would call a man.[22]

The problem of the flood is not of great difficulty, because on the one hand there is geological evidence which is sometimes interpreted as pointing to a universal flood, and on the other hand the universal statements of Gen. 6–8 may be equally figurative with those found all over Scripture (Gen. 41: 57; Acts 2: 5 etc.). They need not be taken to mean more than that the whole *inhabited* earth was deluged, which at a sufficiently early period in the history of mankind (very likely in connection with the last ice-age, which ended at about 10,000 B.C.) is easily credible. The problem of creation, however, cannot be so summarily dealt with. The conclusions of scientists are here, of course, at their most uncertain, because they are here dealing with unique events at the remotest period of history, but there appears to be fairly general agreement that some sort of biological evolution has taken place (though whether natural selection has played an important part in it, and whether the gap between species and species can be satisfactorily filled by this means, seem to be open questions still). This obviously cannot be reconciled with creation in six 24-hour days, at however early a period in history. Genesis 1 is undoubtedly to be regarded as history in some sense, since it opens and sets the scene for that historical revelation and redemption which is the subject of the Bible. But is it literal history, or history that relates in a compressed and figurative form, intelligible in all ages, what is wholly outside the experience of man? It must not be said that the latter suggestion is simply an evasion, and that everyone up to the last century took Genesis 1 literally, for in the first place this is not in fact true (Philo and Augustine are among those who for differing reasons preferred a figurative interpretation), and in the second place the wide acceptance of the literal interpretation may not have been due so much to the demands of the biblical narrative as to old popular ideas of the smallness of the universe, the brevity of history etc., which in this particular were not seriously disturbed until the last century. Actually, there is a good deal in the Bible which should in any age have made readers pause before adopting a purely literal interpretation of Genesis 1, and especially these three facts: (i) Not only light but days, with mornings and evenings, begin on Day One, whereas the sun is not created till Day Four. (ii) On a literal interpretation, Genesis 1 cannot be altogether reconciled with Genesis 2. Thus, in 2: 5–6 the earth is pictured as needing irrigation when, in terms of the previous chapter, literally interpreted, it has only a matter of hours before emerged from the waters. (iii) No end to the seventh day is mentioned, as to the others. The significance of this is brought out in the New Testament, where we learn that the seventh day (God's sabbath) is still continuing (John 5: 17; Heb. 4: 3–10). The obvious conclusion to draw is that we are not dealing with periods of twenty-four hours. If the wholly literal interpretation is to be abandoned, it is not at once clear what we should substitute, though N. H. Ridderbos's book *Is there a Conflict between Genesis One and Natural Science?* (English translation, Grand Rapids Michigan, Eerdmans, 1957), despite its extravagances, may point the way forward.

The Bible is much more closely connected with history than

with natural science, since Christianity is essentially a historical religion. It is always possible, of course, that where historical evidence from secular sources conflicts with the biblical narrative, it is the latter which is right. And Evangelicals would consider that in judging the probabilities in such cases the doctrine of inspiration must be taken into account. Since Scripture is reliable down to its details, according to our Lord and his apostles, and since they explicitly extend inspiration to the historical narratives, there is a great presumption against Scripture having erred in any case of conflict with extra-biblical evidence. Of course, it is common today for theologians to admit that Scripture errs in historical matters, and to say that this makes no difference, since Scripture is not really intended to be history. But we need to be very wary of taking such an attitude, as C. H. Dodd (in his *History and the Gospel* and the introduction to his *Historical Tradition in the Fourth Gospel*) and C. K. Barrett (in his *Luke the Historian*) warn us. For though the interests of the biblical writers are religious, they are treating of a historical religion. History, not essentially different from that written today, was written also in the ancient world, especially in Greece and Rome, and Josephus furnishes us with a good first century link between Hebrew and Greek historiography. It is quite clear that Josephus considered the Old Testament narratives to be history in the Greek and modern sense, and there is no reason to think that the evangelists —contemporaries of Josephus, and continuing the tradition of the Old Testament historians—would have found Greek historiography any more alien to their thinking than Josephus did.

The last class of difficulties to be faced, and the most intangible, consists of difficulties raised by the intellectual temper of the age, that is to say, prejudices. Quite apart from those whose thinking is avowedly or essentially non-Christian, and who will naturally reject the inspiration of Scripture on subjective (usually rationalistic) grounds, there are large numbers of Christians today whose thinking has been so conditioned by the sort of biblical criticism which prevails in this country that it is very difficult for them to conceive that inspiration is a tenable belief. Has not biblical criticism proved that it is not true? they will often ask. The fact is that biblical criticism of the type most familiar to us has not proved but assumed that inspiration is not true. The science of biblical criticism is also pursued by those who assume that inspiration *is* true, and in Holland, Norway, the United States and South Africa, as well as among Roman Catholics, this school of thought is strong. No one who had studied biblical criticism in these circles would make the mistake of thinking that it had proved inspiration to be a false doctrine: they would be more likely to make the opposite mistake of thinking that it had proved inspiration to be a true one.

THE PRACTICAL VALUE OF THE DOCTRINE

It will be clear after all we have said that Evangelicals consider themselves bound to embrace the doctrine of biblical inspiration and infallibility quite apart from any practical value it may have. They are committed to it out of loyalty to Christ, as being part of the Christian gospel which Christ and his apostles taught. But this is not to say that it is without practical value. For what we need is not only God's revelation in history and records of it, as Professor Hanson stressed, but reliable records. And this means not only early records, but records which will not misunderstand or misinterpret the revelation they record. Modern Liberal criticism is constantly telling us that the biblical records are not early enough for us to be certain of the things they record, and it goes without saying that, however early they are, the fallibility of the writers may on Liberal premises have distorted the revelation quite beyond recognition. It is all-important to have reliable records. Ideally we want God's own record of his revelation. And this is what, as Evangelicals believe, he has given us in the inspired Scriptures.[23]

NOTES

[1] On both see W. Goode, *The Divine Rule of Faith and Practice* (2nd edition, London, Jackson, 1853); A. M'Caul, *Testimonies to the Divine Authority and Inspiration of the Holy Scriptures, as taught by the Church of England* (London, Rivingtons, 1862), and C. S. Carter, *The Reformers and Holy Scripture* (London, Thynne and Jarvis, 1928).

[2] See especially M. Reu, *Luther and the Scriptures* (Columbus Ohio, Wartburg, 1944), and with regard to Calvin, J. Murray, *Calvin on Scripture and Divine Sovereignty* (Grand Rapids Michigan, Baker, 1960), and K. S. Kantzer in J. F. Walvoord (ed.), *Inspiration and Interpretation* (Grand Rapids Michigan, Eerdmans, 1957).

[3] See, for example, his *Life and Letters*, by J. O. Johnston (London etc., Longmans, Green and Co., 1904), pp. 371, 382.

[4] In P. J. Thompson and H. E. Symonds, *The Inspiration and Inerrancy of the Bible* (London, S.P.C.K., 1939).

[5] *The Resurrection of the Bible* (Westminster, Dacre, 1940).

[6] *Unity, Uniformity and the English Church* (London, Mowbray, 1961).

[7] As was pointed out in discussion, a few ancient writers suggest that allegorical exegesis is a means of dealing with the difficult statements of Scripture, and are willing that the allegorical meaning should take the place of the literal in these cases. Such are Philo, Origen and Bede. It should be noted, however, that they are arguing in the interests of allegorical exegesis, not biblical infallibility, which they regard as axiomatic. And allegorical exegesis seems on the whole to have been regarded as having only limited usefulness in dealing with biblical difficulties. Most of the passages which perplex us perplexed the Fathers, and they do not normally use allegorical exegesis as a solution.

[8] This point is forcefully made by J. I. Packer in his reply to Hebert's book on Fundamentalism. But the same criticism applies to all these other writers as well, and to many less distinguished.

[9] The book is not written in Greek, as its title might suggest, but in French, and it has in any case been several times translated into English.

[10] *Against Apion* 1: 7–8. For other proofs of Josephus's attitude, see W. Sanday, *Inspiration* (London, Longmans, Green & Co., 1893), pp. 84–5.

[11] Extravagances of individual writers, such as Philo's psychology of inspiration, were not essential to the idea of infallibility, and find no echo in the New Testament.

[12] See his essay in *Lux Mundi*, where he first broached his theory.

[13] See Berkouwer's *Person of Christ* (English translation, Grand Rapids Michigan, Eerdmans, 1954) and Mascall's *Christ, the Christian and the Church* (London etc., Longmans, Green & Co., 1946).

[14] The kenotic interpretation of 2 Cor. 8: 9 and Phil. 2: 7 is arbitrary and in context untenable (see commentaries). Supporting evidence has been sought in Mark 13: 32, but any ignorance experienced by the incarnate Word in his human consciousness must have been voluntary, and it is one thing for him to be ignorant of a matter on which he declined to speak, another thing for him to be ignorant of matters on which he deliberately exercised his mission as Teacher. The truly ignorant and therefore unreliable instructor is the one who, unlike our Lord, is ignorant of the limits of his knowledge. Incidentally, to appeal to a few texts in order to prove in the end that individual texts are unreliable is a curious sort of logic!

[15] *The Person of Christ in New Testament Teaching* (London, Macmillan, 1958).

[16] The bizarre character of this attitude—that in historical and scientific matters we know enough to reject our Lord's statements, but in religious matters, where we do not know enough, we must accept them—is itself remarkable enough. It looks more like a provisional assent to his teaching than real faith.

[17] As we know from Josephus (*Antiquities* 13: 10: 5–6; 13: 15: 5; 13: 16: 1–2; 18: 1: 3), the Pharisees were the great teachers of the people, and had much more influence with them than the Sadducees. Note too how the scribes (Scripture-experts) are in the New Testament almost exclusively linked with the Pharisees.

[18] For proof of this, see J. I. Packer, *Fundamentalism and the Word of God* (London, I.V.F., 1958), appendix 1.

[19] *The Kingdom of Christ* (Everyman edition), vol. 2, p. 149.

[20] It is worth turning up this story to read it in Burgon's inimitable English—*Inspiration and Interpretation* (Oxford etc., Parker, 1861), pp. 64–6.

[21] Both in regard to this class of difficulties and the following it is worth remembering that some of them may be due to an imperfect understanding of the biblical text. Many old difficulties have been cleared away by our growing knowledge of the languages and background of the Bible, and as this growth of knowledge is still continuing, it will probably clear away some of our present difficulties also.

[22] On the question of the genealogies, see J. C. Whitcomb and H. M. Morris, *The Genesis Flood* (Philadelphia, Presbyterian and Reformed, 1961), appendix 2.

[23] It is sometimes objected that even if the Scriptures *were* inspired and infallible, the fact would have no practical value because of our fallibility as interpreters and because of textual uncertainties. The usual answer to this objection, and a sufficient one, is that in our interpretation of the existing text we can at least hope to approximate to the truth, provided the original text was reliable: but if to our fallibility as interpreters and an uncertain text is added an unreliable original, our hope of attaining to the truth becomes a very forlorn one indeed. Thus the objection falls to the ground, and the practical value of the inspiration and infallibility of Scripture remains unimpaired. Incidentally, it is worth noting with what confidence our Lord and his apostles treat the existing texts as the word of God, and commend them to the study of the Church. It is not, of course, possible in a paper of this length to deal at all fully with the questions of text and interpretation, which are in any case not our present subject. For the same reasons nothing has been said about the canon.

SACRIFICE IN THE EUCHARIST

by

H. BENEDICT GREEN

SACRIFICE IN THE EUCHARIST

THE sub-committee of the Lambeth Conference of 1958 which examined the Book of Common Prayer was pleased to endorse, as a reconciliation of conflicting views on the subject of eucharistic sacrifice, the following words of the late Fr. A. G. Hebert:

'The eucharistic Sacrifice, that storm-centre of controversy, is finding in our day a truly evangelical expression from the "catholic" side, when it is insisted that the sacrificial action is not any sort of re-immolation of Christ, nor a sacrifice additional to his one Sacrifice, but a participation in it. The true celebrant is Christ the High-Priest, and the Christian people are assembled as members of his Body to present before God his Sacrifice, and to be themselves offered up in Sacrifice through their union with him. This, however, involves a repudiation of certain mediaeval developments, notably the habitual celebration of the Eucharist without the Communion of the people, or the notion that the offering of the Eucharist is the concern of the individual priest rather than of the assembled church; and, above all, any idea that in the Eucharist we offer a sacrifice to propitiate God. We offer it only because he has offered the one Sacrifice, once for all, in which we need to participate.' [1]

There is much in this with which to agree; but it may be questioned whether the charity of its intention is matched by the rigour of its logic, and whether therefore it is adequate to bridge the gap between such statements as, on one side:

'The priest did offer Christ for quick and dead, to have remission of pain or guilt' (Article XXXI): or—in the expanded form offered by Fr. Francis Clark:

'The belief that Jesus Christ is daily offered on the Church's altars for the welfare of the living and the dead, his body and blood really present under the appearances of bread and wine, the belief that he has instituted a priestly order of men sharing in his own sacerdotal power and authority through whom he continues to offer his propitiatory sacrifice to the eternal Father, in order to apply to mankind in every age and place the benefits of redemption and salvation won for them by his death upon the cross— this is for catholics one of the fundamentals of their faith' (Francis

Clark, S.J., *Eucharistic Sacrifice and the Reformation,* 1960, p. 3) and on the other side:

'The Eucharist is the divinely instituted remembrance of Christ's sacrifice, and in it God gives and the Church receives the fruits of that sacrifice, the Body and Blood of Christ. In virtue of this, and only so, the Church is enabled to make that offering of praise, thanksgiving, and self-oblation which (apart from the alms) is the only sacrifice actually offered in the Eucharist. Only as united to Christ in his death and resurrection through receiving the Body and Blood of Christ is the Church able to offer itself acceptably to the Father.' (*The Fulness of Christ,* a report presented to the Archbishop of Canterbury by a group of evangelical theologians, 1950, p. 32.)

When the opposed positions are stated as intransigently as this, it is neither practicable nor honest to paper over the gap between them. They are hardly to be reconciled as they stand; and it is not really the business of a writer who represents neither the evangelical nor the Roman Catholic position to make concessions on behalf of either. He can but offer criticisms of the arguments used by both, and suggest that neither position is as closed as these particular defenders make it look. It must be added that those who adopt a 'catholic' position outside the Roman Catholic Church do not necessarily commit themselves even to representative statements from within it—deeply as they are indebted to the theologians who have given a 'new look' to Roman Catholic eucharistic theology in the past fifty years.

The way in which Fr. Clark has argued his case as a whole is a model of controversial courtesy. But his initial statement of his own theological position is not intended to be conciliatory, as is shown by the provocative way in which he has paraphrased in it the statement contained in the Anglican Article. How far the wording of that Article is responsible for his apparent restriction of all sacrificial activity in the eucharist to the ministerial priesthood, it is impossible to say; but he could have shown, had he wished, without any departure from the official teaching of his own Church, a much more explicit recognition that the eucharist is the sacrifice of the whole Church, and that the admittedly crucial and indispensable role of the ministerial priesthood is to be understood within the context of that; as Professor Ratcliff has put it,[2] 'the celebrant has received the priesthood for exercise within the *plebs sancta Dei* and not apart from it.' Hebert's remarks on this subject are clearly right, as far as they go; and they certainly go no further in emphasizing the priestly character of the whole body of Christians than does Fr. Yves Congar in his important book *Lay People in the Church*.

Fr. Clark comes nearer to the heart of the controversy with his statement that 'Jesus Christ is daily offered.' He does not of course mean, and insists that the mediaeval theologians of whom his book is very largely a defence did not mean, that Christ is slain afresh. It seems on his showing that the idea that something of a destructive character is done to Christ in the Mass originated with counter-Reformation writers, and that they let themselves be driven into this trap by the reformers' insistence on the equivalence of sacrifice with death (since without shedding of blood there is no remission). The mediaeval writers mostly equated Christ's sacrifice with his passion, but they did *not* accept the implication that the Mass, because it is a sacrifice, is a fresh passion; they saw it rather as a mystic commemoration of his one passion. Their difficulty, and their successors', lay in explaining satisfactorily how this commemoration of a sacrifice is itself a sacrifice, and in what sense the formula 'Christ is offered' is applicable to it.

The source of the formula, and of the difficulties to which it has given rise, lies in the belief that in the eucharist the *consecrated* elements are offered to God. The roots of this lie a long way back. The section *Unde et memores* of the Canon of the Roman Mass contains the words 'we offer here to thy glorious majesty, of thine own gifts and bounties, . . . the holy bread of eternal life and the cup of everlasting salvation'[3]; and since this section *follows* the institution narrative which is regarded as effecting the consecration, the substance of the offering is understood as the consecrated elements, the body and blood of Christ, or, more briefly, Christ himself. St. Ambrose, who used a form of the Roman Canon, is the earliest writer who explicitly treats the words of institution as the moment of consecration (though, as Br. George Every has shown, the practical implications of his view were not fully accepted until the early middle ages).[4] But, early as this attestation is, there are indications that at a still earlier date the words in question denoted the *unconsecrated* elements (e.g. *de tuis donis ac datis,* and the repeated use of the neuter plural *haec* to refer to them). Certainly the construction later placed upon these words makes the Roman rite in its present form unique in Christendom; the eastern rites know nothing of it, but locate the moment of consecration in the epiclesis at the end of the eucharistic prayer, so that all expressions of oblation refer to the unconsecrated elements. And Bishop Aulen has recently emphasized [5] that Luther's objection to sacrifice in the eucharist was entirely directed against the idea of offering Christ; believing as he did in real and objective presence of Christ, he understood this as the presence of Christ *in his sacrificed state.* There has been a similar tendency in some Roman Catholic thinking on this subject since World War I. The account of the Mass given, for instance, by Canon Eugene Masure is, broadly, that it makes present under visible signs of bread and wine the sacrifice of Christ.[6] That this is hardly the same as to 'offer Christ' and certainly not what the words immediately suggest has not yet been sufficiently considered; and the liturgical implications of such a position have still to be tackled. But the convergence of views is significant, and takes us back to the New Testament itself. For the seed of the doctrine of eucharistic sacrifice is to be found in the narrative of institution; body and blood in separation signify, as Jeremias has shown,[7] sacrificial entities—the body of the victim and the blood drained from it. But though the bread and wine are identified with these, it is nowhere said that they are *offered.*

To speak of Christ in his sacrificed state brings us to the central issue in this controversy—the meaning of sacrifice. Fr. Clark assumes that Christ 'continues to offer his propitiatory sacrifice to the eternal Father.' The authors of *The Fulness of Christ* see Christ's sacrifice as the object of remembrance, and the Church's present sacrifice as entirely distinct from, though dependent on it. Hebert sees it as something in which Christians can participate. How many senses of the word are here in play? Does *sacrifice* denote a single act or an abiding reality? A few distinctions and precisions will not be out of order at this point. It is necessary, first of all, to insist that sacrifice is not in itself necessarily connected with either death or sin. The part played by death is not central, since not all ritual sacrifices were of animals (there was also the cereal offering and, in some systems, the drink-offering too), and when they were, the death was only one stage, and that a preparatory one, in making over to God that which was offered to him. The end of the process was not that the creature should die, but that God should accept it. (This was seen by St. Bernard when he said of our Lord: *non mors, sed voluntas placuit ipsius morientis*—'it was not the death that was pleasing, but the will of him that died'—and his remark only echoes the use made in the Epistle to the Hebrews of the great passage from Ps. 40: 'Sacrifices and offerings thou hast not desired, but a body hast thou prepared for me; in burnt offerings and sin offerings thou hast taken no pleasure. Then I said, "Lo, I have come to do thy will, O God," as it is written of me in the roll of the book.' [8]) Again, the category of sacrifice embraced far more than the sin-offering; it included the thank-offering and the peace-offering and the commemorative sacrifice of the passover. (St. Augustine was not far wrong in defining sacrifice as 'every action done that we may be joined to God in holy fellowship' [9]—a purpose which may be fulfilled by various kinds of action, of which expiation for sin is only one, and not in all circumstances the dominant one.) When the sin-offering was offered in Judaism, it was as a preliminary to worship, concerned with the removal of disqualifications from worshipping, and not as the worship itself. The entire argument of the Epistle to the Hebrews rests upon this distinction (see especially Heb. 9: 13–14).

If these two things are true of sacrifice in general, what light do they throw on the sacrifice of Christ in particular? The New Testament represents Christ's sacrifice as our sin-offering, as the following texts illustrate:

'Christ died for our sins according to the scriptures' (1 Cor. 15: 4).

'Christ gave himself up for us, an offering and a sacrifice to God for an odour of a sweet smell' (Eph. 5: 3).

'Christ, who through the eternal Spirit offered himself without blemish to God' (Heb. 9: 13).

'. . . this he did once for all, when he offered up himself' (ibid., 7: 27).

The offering was made once for all, in time; but though it involved his death, it was the sacrifice, objectively, of himself. It was consummated in his death, but can it be said that it began

55

then? For he was not a short time dying. Did it then begin as he was nailed to the cross? But was not his will to go through with it fortified in Gethsemane? And did he not signify its meaning to the disciples in the upper room? And do not the gospels rightly see his entry into Jerusalem as the beginning of his passion? And was there not a moment in his ministry when he deliberately turned and set his face to go to Jerusalem? And did he not at the beginning of that ministry accept baptism at the hands of John so that he might fulfil all righteousness? These are all prior to the death, but still part of the sacrifice. Though it was his death that consummated the sacrifice and made it irrevocable and revealed its full cost, there was no point in the incarnate life which was pre-sacrificial.

Are we therefore to say that the sacrifice is going on still? That would be to go back on the *ephapax,* to compromise its once-for-all character; what Christ *did* was complete with the last breath on Calvary. Certainly the resurrection and ascension and heavenly session of Christ are related to the sacrificial death, but not as though they continued it in a straight line. They are the indications that God has accepted the offering; and whereas the offering was an event in time, the acceptance of it is an abiding reality of the heavenly places, where Christ, who was dead, is alive for ever-more. Christ's risen life and glorified state, though rooted in the cross, belong to the eternal here and now. That Christ offered himself once for all, yet remains from that time a priest for ever, is the double theme of the Epistle to the Hebrews, and the two aspects are combined within the single image of the Lamb in the midst of the heavenly assembly in the Apocalypse, who is the Lamb as it had been slain. The finished work of his sacrificial death is somehow contained in the ever-present reality of his accepted sacrifice, which is, of course, himself.

We must therefore distinguish, with Masure[10] (to whose exposition I am deeply indebted) between the sacrifice *as offered,* the past event completed at a point in time, Christ's finished work, and the sacrifice *as accepted,* the present and continuing reality, in which Christians may in some sense share. This is a far more satisfactory account of the matter than any theory of the continuing sacrificial *activity* of Christ. There has been a tendency in some quarters to speak of the heavenly intercession of Christ as though his atoning work consisted of his passion on earth *plus* his pleading in heaven, the eucharist being regarded as a commemoration or representation of the former and a participation in the latter. This was a way out of the dilemma 'either recollection or repetition of the sacrifice' which was much in favour both with seventeenth century high Anglicans,[11] from whom it passed to the Wesleys and their followers,[12] and with certain post-Tractarian writers.[13] But it lacks biblical foundation. The New Testament does not represent the glorified Christ in the attitude of prayer; the Epistle to the Hebrews speaks of him as *sitting* at the right hand of God.[14] His intercession is not an activity; it consists in the *presence* of his glorified humanity in the heavenly places, while his members are still in the midst of their conflict on earth. To make it an activity, whether of pleading or presentation, unavoidably introduces the idea of something added to the cross, without which the latter is not complete; and the same applies to the eucharist when interpreted along these lines. But to make the accepted sacrifice of Christ sacramentally present is not to add anything to it; it is simply the means whereby the inadequate self-offering of Christians is transfigured by the divine acceptance in union with the altogether final sacrifice of Christ, which is acknowledged to be their only claim to appear before God : 'Nothing in my hand I bring, simply to thy cross I cling.'

But the doctrine of the full, perfect and sufficient sacrifice of Christ for men does not prevent the writers of the New Testament from using sacrificial language about various attitudes and activities of Christians, e.g. :

praise and thanksgiving: Heb. 13 : 15.

faith: Phil. 2 : 17.

self-oblation: Rom. 12 : 1.

sacrificial service of others: Heb. 13 : 16.

the offerings of money produced by this: Phil. 4 : 18 (and note the close parallel with the language used in Eph. 5 : 2 of the sacrifice of Christ).

And in Rom. 15 : 16 St. Paul describes himself as 'a minister of Christ Jesus to the Gentiles in the priestly service of the gospel of God, so that the offering of the Gentiles may be acceptable, sanctified by the Holy Spirit.' This implies that the Gentiles are in some sense offered to God, or, more properly, that they offer themselves, through the ministerial activity of Paul.

Here then we have two things, the sacrifice of Christ, and the sacrifices of Christians. Are they so disparate that there can be no connection between them? Do they proceed on parallel lines without ever converging? Hardly so, if both are to be called by the same name; hardly, if both are the consequence of Christ's sharing of our human nature. Sacrifice is, by definition, a God-directed activity of men; Christ's own sacrifice was itself the work of Christ as man; if it was only the Son of God who could offer to the Father the sacrifice acceptable to him, he had still to become man in order to make the oblation—and the force of this is not reversed or weakened by the paradox of the divine initiative through which the victim of the atoning sacrifice was the Lamb which God himself had provided. Christ shared our humanity and in it offered on our behalf the sacrifice which his perfect humanity did not need, the atonement for the world's sin; we who are a new creation in Christ share in his glorified humanity and in it make through him that offering of ourselves, our lives and our labours which his sacrifice alone has made possible. We receive from him what we cannot produce of ourselves, but our reception of it enables us to perform in him the Father's good pleasure. We do not simply imitate his sacrifice—that would be Pelagian—nor can we be said to respond to it; for if sacrifice is a God-directed activity of men, then it is God who responds to it. But Christ enables us to be one with him, not only in his humanity, but in its obedience.

If then Christ's sacrifice has abrogated the sacrifices of the Jewish law, it does not follow, for the New Testament writers, that there can be no further sacrifice of any kind. Christ's is not the sacrifice to end all sacrifices—though it *is* the sin-offering to end all sin-offerings. What remain are 'spiritual' sacrifices—as opposed to the 'ritual' sacrifices of the old law, which rested on the letter and not on the spirit, of which the essential part was the external action and the material object on which it was executed. But 'spiritual' is not here opposed to 'material' as such —what after all could be more material than a human body or a coin of the currency?—nor therefore to the signification of spiritual attitudes by physical actions and material objects.

It has still nevertheless to be established that what the New Testament has to say about the sacrifices of Christians is applicable to the eucharist itself. Most Christians would agree that it is in some sense; they differ about the relation between the Church's oblation and the sacramental gift. For the catholic the oblation comes first and the sacramental gift is the seal and consequence of its acceptance; for the evangelical the gift comes first and the oblation (where admitted) is the Church's response to its reception. Thus we read in *The Fulness of Christ:* 'In virtue of this [sc. the reception of the body and blood of Christ] and only so, the Church is enabled to make that offering of praise, thanksgiving and self-oblation which (apart from the alms) is the only sacrifice actually offered in the eucharist.' The question at issue is whether the eucharistic action has primarily a Godward or a manward direction.

In favour of the latter alternative the evangelical would advance three main arguments: (i) The words of St. Paul in 1 Cor. 11: 26, 'For as often as you eat this bread and drink the cup, you proclaim the Lord's death until he comes.' (ii) That the whole scheme of redemption follows the pattern of divine initiative followed by human response, and the eucharist may be expected to conform to this. (iii) That sacraments are by definition gifts of God to which we respond, and the eucharist is a sacrament.

(i) If I may repeat what I have written elsewhere [15]: 'It is correctly urged that elsewhere the word "proclaim" (*katangellō*) is used always of the proclamation of the gospel to men—correctly, that is, except for one instance in the Epistle to the Romans, where St. Paul says "I thank my God through Jesus Christ for you all, that your faith is proclaimed throughout the whole world." This cannot mean that the Roman Christians' faith is preached as part of the gospel; it must mean that it is everywhere known, spoken of and rejoiced at. The word can therefore bear a more general sense. Now the use of the word in St. Paul's eucharistic passage is unique in that the proclamation is made, not by apostles to the unconverted, but by all the communicants—to whom? Not to the heathen, for none would have been present; nor, surely, to each other, for that would only have been to make people aware of something they were already taking action about, which is hardly what is commonly meant by preaching the gospel. It is hard to resist the conclusion that the word is used with a less precise meaning, such as might be conveyed by the English *celebrate*.

When we celebrate, e.g., the Nativity of our Lord at Christmas, we do not directly pass on the good news to each other, as if it were a novelty; we remind both ourselves and each other of it by our common observance. Nor do we expressly convey it to the outside world, though our observance will make it plain enough what we are about. Nor yet do we presume to put God in mind of what he knows so much better than we; but the first and foremost part of our celebration is nevertheless to thank him for it. Every commemoration of an event in which God was active must have this Godward reference, without thereby excluding the manward one.' It may be added that I Cor. 11 : 26 is St. Paul's own gloss on the preceding verses, which he is presumably quoting from the liturgical tradition with which he was familiar, and in particular on the refrain 'Do this for my *anamnesis*'; *katangellō* probably expresses what St. Paul himself understood by *anamnesis*. As Fr. Audet has shown,[16] the meaning in this context of *anamnesis* is connected with the form of the Jewish *herākāh* or thanksgiving which, after naming God, recalls the acts for which his name is to be praised; e.g. 'Bless the Lord, O my soul; and all that is within me bless his holy name! . . . who forgives all your iniquity, who heals all your diseases . . . '[17] Such a form would unquestionably have been used over the bread and the cup by our Lord, and the usage would have been continued by his disciples; out of it the Church's eucharistic prayer has developed. The hypothesis that St. Paul has it in mind when writing to the Corinthians fits the evidence better than any other; and implies a Godward reference both in the Lord's command and the apostle's gloss on it.

(ii) It is perfectly true that God's dealing with man follows the pattern of divine initiative followed by human response, but this does not necessarily mean that the eucharistic action itself covers the whole of the pattern. Its dominant note is thanksgiving; as we have seen, the Lord's action in giving thanks has become the eucharistic prayer of the Church's liturgy, and this is the only substantive prayer of the rite and therefore determines the direction of the entire action (though that has not prevented a number of Christian liturgies, including the Roman Mass and the Communion Office of the Book of Common Prayer from seriously obscuring its character as a thanksgiving). But thanksgiving is essentially a response, presupposing something that has gone before. In the context of the liturgy this is the proclamation of the word; in the person of the worshipper it is his baptism.

The eucharistic liturgy is normally introduced by a service of the word with reading from scripture and, ideally, a sermon; the thanksgiving and the eucharistic action to which it is central follow as a response to this. God speaks to us in the word; we respond in thanksgiving and self-oblation, and Christ crowns this response with the gift of himself.

On this view word and sacrament are not parallel in their operation, as the reformers thought, so much as complementary. The Reformation view is not in fact early; there is really nothing to correspond to it in the New Testament (which does not speak at all of *sacraments* as such, though it has plenty to say of baptism and the eucharist in their own right). An illuminating clue to the origin of the parallelism is provided by Fr. J. A. Jungmann.[18] He draws attention to the change that came over the western Church's attitude to the eucharistic liturgy in the Dark Ages, when the ancient conception of the action as an *eucharistia* rising from men to God came to be eclipsed and superseded by that of a *bona gratia* (i.e. the consecration) descending from God to men. Once this way of looking at the eucharist had established itself, it was only natural that the word preached, when the cardinal importance of that was rediscovered at the Reformation, should also be understood, in effect, as a *bona gratia,* and even that the word and the sacraments should be regarded as strictly parallel ways of effecting the same thing. But the result was an oversimplification of their real relationship.

Much the same may be said of the relation of the two great sacraments to one another. That they are parallel in a great many respects there is no need to deny; both are concerned with the covenant, with the death of Christ, with the forgiveness of sins, with the Body of Christ, with sonship, with the anticipation of the kingdom. But at the same time it is true (1) that baptism is performed once for all, and so is concerned with establishing a relationship, whereas the eucharist is intended to be continually repeated, and is therefore concerned with renewing that relationship; (2) that baptism is for the initiation and incorporation of the individual, while the eucharist is properly the action of the whole Church, and it is *qua* member that the individual takes part in it; (3) (what amounts to much the same) that the subject of baptism is an unsanctified sinner, of whom only repentance and faith are required as antecedent conditions, whereas it is required of the communicant at the eucharist that he be not only a penitent believer, but a baptized person. In view of this it is extraordinary to find the authors of *The Fulness of Christ* writing: 'Only as united with Christ in his death and resurrection *through receiving the Body and Blood of Christ* is the Church able to offer itself acceptably to the Father' (italics mine). It is an elementary truth that the sacrament in which we die and rise with Christ is not the eucharist but baptism; and it should be equally obvious that the sacrament which gives free access to the throne of God is likewise not the eucharist but baptism. As the Epistle to the Hebrews puts it: 'Therefore, brethren, since we have confidence to enter the sanctuary by the blood of Jesus, by the new and living way which he opened for us through the curtain, that is, through his flesh, and since we have a great high priest over the house of God, let us draw near with a true heart in full assurance of faith, with our hearts sprinkled clean from an evil conscience, and our bodies washed with pure water' [19]—the last two phrases evidently referring to the inward and outward parts of the sacrament of baptism respectively. I have said that the argument of this Epistle depends on the distinction between the sin-offering which removes disqualifications for worship, and the worship itself; in the sacramental order it is baptism that corresponds to the sin-offering, and the eucharist that corresponds to the worship. And for the early Christians Christian initiation consisted of the two together—baptismal rebirth and incorporation into the ecclesial body of Christ leading to eucharistic worship and participation in the sacramental body of Christ. The two sacraments are complementary—baptism the once-for-all: the eucharist the continual becoming-what-you-are. Every eucharist presupposes that the participants are already Christ's through baptism; they come as sinners, certainly, but as *justified* sinners. Only in the light of this can we answer the question whether they may, in any particular eucharist, worthily offer themselves to God before they have, *on that occasion*, received Christ.

(iii) The above argument largely disposes of the suggestion that

62

the account of the sacramental action in baptism and the eucharist can be reduced to a single overall formula. But, quite apart from this, it is an oversimplification to say that sacraments are simply divine gifts to which we respond. The divine gift is itself bestowed at the prayers of the Church (the basic text for all sacramental theology is 'Whatever you ask the Father in my name, he will give it you'), and it can only be received fruitfully by the individual if he receives it with the requisite dispositions of penitence and faith, which are antecedent, not a response, to the sacramental gift itself. (That is not to bring back human works into the picture; it is true that the *ex opere operato* principle is implicit in the text I have just cited from John 14: 13, but the words 'in my name' certify that the act is that of Christ in his Church, and therefore may not be equated with those works of men or works of the law that are opposed to saving faith. There is no fundamental opposition between *sola fide* and *ex opere operato* when both are properly understood.) This means that the question of divine initiative and human response is more complicated than the traditional evangelical presentation of it allows for. Behind the sacramental order lies the creation and redemption of man and the establishment of the Church of God. Divine initiative comes before human response in principle, but sacraments belong to an order in which they are already interacting; the order of the incarnate Christ, who acts towards us both as God and man. As God, he brings God to us, and as man he leads us to God. God speaks to us in the gospel of Christ; we respond in faith, and our faith culminates in our baptism, in which Christ unites us with himself in his death and resurrection, and thereby brings us to the privilege of sonship. God's word to us is reaffirmed in the proclamation at the worship of the Church; we respond in thanksgiving, in which our union with Christ is renewed. The culmination which Christ bestows in either case is subsequent and not prior to our initial response.

For a similar reason an absolute opposition of *sacrament* in which God gives to men and *sacrifice* in which man is supposed to give to God (implied in my too-neat contrast of the catholic and the evangelical attitudes) is not easily applicable to the eucharist. St. Thomas Aquinas said of it '*hoc sacramentum est sacramentum et sacrificium,*' and a commentator [20] has said that this does not mean that the eucharist is partly sacrament and partly sacrifice, but wholly both. That is, the sacramental feeding is properly understood as the consummation of the sacrificial action, while the sacramental character (that of being conveyed through and under visible signs) attaches not only to what God gives to men, but to the conditions under which what man (in Christ) brings to God is acceptable to him.

What account, finally, is to be given of the complete eucharistic action? Let us observe the traditional divisions.

(1) The offertory.

Despite widespread assumptions to the contrary, it cannot be taken as self-evident that the offertory represents the offering of ourselves. It is the preliminary to the eucharistic offering rather than a part of the offering itself: the provision of the material elements without which it cannot be offered. But this much at any rate may be said:

(a) Bread and wine belong to the created order, and the eucharist gives thanks for it.

(b) They are also the product of man's labour upon God's gifts, and the act of bringing them has an obvious analogy with the Jewish offering of firstfruits; if God does not now require of us sacrifices of this sort as such, he still demands our thanks, of which they are the visible token, and we still need to acknowledge our dependence on him.

(c) They are the elements which Christ has commanded to be used, and the bringing of them is therefore an act of obedience and representative of all our obedience.

(d) We do not send but bring them in person, and this cannot but imply an association of ourselves with what is presented to God.

(2) The eucharistic prayer.

This is, as we have seen, the only substantive prayer of the rite, and is to be understood as:

(a) The prayer of *thanksgiving,* or rather of glorification of God for his mighty acts in creation and redemption which it recalls.

(b) Since the thanksgiving is at the same time a thankoffering, done with concrete objects, bread and wine, it is also a prayer of *offering* of the Church's gifts, and through them of itself, in union with the already accepted sacrifice of Christ.

(c) Only thus can it be called the prayer of *consecration,* which is to be understood as the transformation of the Church's offering by the divine acceptance, so that the bread and wine become the effective signs of the body and blood of Christ, making his accepted sacrifice sacramentally present. 'The Church's offering is effaced, in the presence of the unique and perfect sacrifice of Christ.' [21]

(3) The Communion.

This is of course the climax of the whole rite, which can be described as a communion in sacrifice, or as a sacrifice only consummated in communion. The Church's gifts are only identified with the accepted sacrifice of Christ in order that by their means its members may be identified with it also—that is, accepted in Christ. Their offering of themselves, which the gifts, in some sense, symbolize, is imperfect until transcended by union with the accepted sacrifice of Christ. This is one reason why the catholic holds fast to the doctrine of the transformation of the elements; it actually safeguards the truth that in this transaction we are nothing and Christ is everything. But there is a further reason. At the heart of the eucharistic mystery lie the body and the blood. If these are not in fact present in the midst, but only conveyed by means of the outward sign to the individual communicant—if he is spiritually fed with an absent body—the result is bound to be a religious individualism singularly inappropriate to the sacrament of unity, in which Christians are fed with Christ's body that they may be renewed as Christ's body. 'Because there is one loaf, we who are many are one body, for we are all partakers of the same loaf.' [22]

NOTES

[1] *The Lambeth Conference 1958,* pp. **2.** 84f.

[2] In a paper entitled 'Principles Governing Liturgical Revision,' published in *The World for God,* the Report of the Church Union Eucharistic Congress of 1958, p. 64.

[3] Translation by Dom Gregory Dix, *Shape of the Liturgy,* p. 114 (slightly altered).

[4] See George Every, *The Baptismal Sacrifice,* p. 76, and cf. J. A. Jungmann, *The Mass of the Roman Rite,* I, p. 82. On the whole relation of offering to consecration see George Every, *Basic Liturgy,* especially pp. 8f., 99ff., 109ff., and H. Green, 'A New Look at the Epiclesis' in *Sobornost,* 4: 3 (Summer–Autumn 1960), pp. 105ff.

[5] G. Aulen, *Eucharist and Sacrifice*, 1960, pp. 90ff. See especially p. 91: 'It is the glorified Christ, the one 'everywhere present' who according to his word has connected his presence with the bread and wine, and who thereby actualizes his sacrifice and makes it present.'

[6] See *The Christian Sacrifice* (1932, E.T. 1944); *The Sacrifice of the Mystical Body* (1950; E.T. 1954).

[7] J. Jeremias, *The Eucharistic Words of Jesus* (E.T. 1954), pp. 139ff.

[8] Heb. 10: 5–7.

[9] Augustine, *City of God*, x, 6.

[10] *The Christian Sacrifice*, pp. 154–62, especially p. 162: '. . . there must be no question of making this mystery a separate sacrifice, or even a continuous facsimile of the first, a sort of anniversary of a great event renewed only by way of jubilee commemoration. No! it is the same event which still takes place and never stops: the sitting at the Father's right hand, as defined in the Creed, is simply the mystery of the Ascension considered as static and in the language of time proper to us human beings. But in good theology, without the use of imagery, it is the reception of the glorified Son by the Father, the acceptance which is nothing else than the apotheosis of the victim.'

[11] For the views of e.g., Cosin, Taylor, Bramhall and Thorndike, see C. W. Dugmore, *Eucharistic Doctrine in England from Hooker to Waterland*, pp. 82ff. How far, if at all, they were indebted to the 'French School' of Condren, Olier and Thomassin, of whom Masure is offering a corrected interpretation, is a subject that deserves more study than it has yet received. A possible influence from another quarter is the group of French Reformed divines of whom Pierre du Moulin was the chief; see Max Thurian, *The Eucharistic Memorial*, 2, pp. 87ff.

A famous pictorial representation of this view is the frontispiece to Charles Wheatly's *Rational Illustration of the Book of Common Prayer* (first published 1710), which depicts an Anglican clergyman celebrating the Lord's Supper in the manner customary at that time, and in a cloud above his head the Great High Priest, standing at the north end of the heavenly altar. It should be emphasized that the image of the heavenly altar, of which this school of thought made much, is much older than the seventeenth century, being found in the Roman Canon as in Irenaeus before it; and its scriptural associations are not with the heavenly intercession of Hebrews but with the heavenly worship of the Apocalypse.

[12] The Wesleys turned into verse the teaching and even the wording of *The Christian Sacrament and Sacrifice* by Daniel Brevint (1616–95)—though the author of the account of Brevint in *D.N.B.* says that the Wesleys' adaptation was 'pitched in a somewhat higher key of eucharistic doctrine' than Brevint's works. See J. E. Rattenbury, *The Eucharistic Hymns of John and Charles Wesley*.

[13] e.g. W. Bright, F. W. Puller, and, in an extreme form, F. E. Brightman, whose pamphlet *The Eucharistic Sacrifice* is devastatingly handled in A. G. Mortimer's book of the same title.

[14] That the dying Stephen sees him *standing* need not be pressed against this, in view of the close parallels between the Lucan writings (and especially this section of them) and the Epistle to the Hebrews. Cf. C. P. M. Jones on this subject in *Studies in the Gospels* (ed. D. E. Nineham) and W. Manson, *The Epistle to the Hebrews*.

[15] H. Green, 'The Eucharist in Anglican Controversy,' in *Sobornost*, 3, 18 (Winter 1956), p. 300.

[16] J. P. Audet, 'Literary Forms and Contents of a Normal *eucharistia* in the First Century' in *Studia Evangelica*, 1959, pp. 643ff.

[17] Ps. 103: 1, 2.

[18] *Mass of the Roman Rite*, I, p. 82.

[19] Heb. 10: 19–22.

[20] Dom Gregory Dix in *Laudate*, 1932 (reviewing F. C. N. Hicks, *The Fulness of Sacrifice*).

[21] Max Thurian, Introductory Essay to *The Eucharistic Liturgy of Taizé*, p. 18.

[22] 1 Cor. 10: 17.

LAY SPIRITUALITY

by

MICHAEL HENNELL

LAY SPIRITUALITY

I. IN THE PAST

'LAY SPIRITUALITY' is a term that has quite suddenly come into wide use. I am not certain that I understand its full meaning, but it must at least include the attempt of the lay Christian to say his prayers, read his Bible and take his full part in the life of the worshipping community. It must also include his attempt to maintain his Christian life in face of the pressures of the world. Probably like me, you think that this subject is more the province of the parish priest than of a college principal who has most to do with young men who have ceased to be laymen and are not quite clergymen. However this may be, my approach will probably be different from what an incumbent might say on the same subject; for if he were writing this essay the final section on lay spirituality today would probably be thicker and the middle section, which is historical, thinner.

There is a change in the climate of opinion about the place of the laity in the Church of God. Any one who has met visiting churchmen from U.S.A. or Canada will know how surprised they are that the laity are given so little scope in the Church of England. It has been a major concern of the Roman Catholic Church since the war to rediscover a theology of the laity and Fr. Congar has attempted to define the place, responsibility and function of the laity in the Roman Church alongside the hierarchy. The non-Roman churches on the Continent show a growing concern; the World Council has a department devoted to the laity. In the Church of England there are some signs of movement, with increased use of lay-readers and in the Christian Stewardship movement, but on the whole most people here think of the Church's job as the parson's job, and when a modern journalist comes to take a look at the Church from the outside he writes a book almost solely about the clergy.

Bishop Barry says: 'Even still today the English Protestant layman or nominal Church of England man keeps one foot on the Latin side of the Reformation watershed. He believes in salvation by works. And for all his denunciation of priestcraft he remains an inveterate "sacerdotalist." [1] Religion, he thinks, is the business of the parson,' and of course, it might be added, there are parsons who like it that way; but it is not the way of the New Testament.

69

In the New Testament there is no division between clergy and laity. There is a division in the Old Testament between priests and other members of the Israel of God, and a division between priests and laity very early on in Church History, but in the New Testament there is no such division—all Christians are 'saints,' all Christians are 'priests.' ('Unto him that loveth us, and loosed us from our sins by his blood; and he made us to be a kingdom, to be priests, unto his God and Father' (Rev. 1 : 5, 6) and St. Peter writing of the Church as the new Israel says 'Ye are an elect race, a royal priesthood, a holy nation, a people for God's own possession.' So we might go on.)

Dr. Alec Vidler in a sermon on Christian Priesthood says :

'Lots of Christians do not realize that they are priests. They think only clergymen are priests. They are living far away back in the Old Testament, poor souls. . . . I will give you 5s. for every place in the New Testament you can show me where, when Christians are spoken of, ministers are called priests and not laymen as well. And I will tell you that you can spend the whole of this afternoon pouring over your copy of Cruden's *Concordance*, and I shall not be a penny the poorer.' [2]

The heart of the matter lies in the fact that the word *laos* (from which we get the word 'laity') means people and in the New Testament means the whole people of God. As one writer says 'The two words *kleros* (clergy) and *laos* (laity) appear in the New Testament, but, strange to say, they denote the same people, not different people.' Of course there was a New Testament ministry of presbyter-bishops and deacons, but the difference between them and the rest of God's people was one of function not of status.

How then did the 'laity' become the term used in the church for those members who are not its ordained ministers? The word *kleros* in the New Testament (from which we get the word 'clergy') means portion or inheritance. 1 Peter 5 : 3 A.V. translates 'neither as being lords over God's heritage, the heritage being the whole people of God.' But in the secular life of the Graeco-Roman empire there was a significant difference of meaning. The city state was divided into two sectors 'the *kleros*' or magistrate and the *laos,* the people. This division was taken over into the Church within the first two centuries and was obviously drawn from the practice of civil society. T. M. Lindsay says 'The laity were called *plebs* and the clergy the *ordo*—the names applied to the commons and the senate of the Italian and provincial towns. As the members of the senate or the *ordo* had a special bench, called the consessus, in the basilica or court house, so the clergy had special seats in church. "It is the authority of the Church," says Tertullian, "that makes the difference between the *ordo* and the *plebs*—this and the honour consecrated by the special bench of the *ordo*" ' ³ (T. M. Lindsay, *Church and Ministry in the Early Centuries*, footnote, pp. 245–6).

A further widening of the gulf came with Constantine, for he allowed Christian clergy to enjoy all the rights and exemptions enjoyed by heathen priests. They were free from appearing in the secular courts through benefit of clergy, they did not have to perform public service in town government or magistracy. In this way they became more distinct as a class. By the twelfth century Canon Law recognized two kinds of Christians—'priests' and 'laymen'—and the line between sacred and secular, which is not drawn in the Bible, was now clearly drawn in the Church. The double-standard of first-class Christians being composed entirely of 'clergy' and second-class of 'laity' is perhaps the most fatal distortion of the Middle Ages. (The laity were really only thought of as Christians on sufferance; they might be saved by doing good and avoiding vice, but the way to save your soul was to become a religious and enter a monastery or nunnery. Even the parish priests were not really on the top level; they were called 'secular clergy.') The division was further accentuated by the new monopoly of education that the clerical class had. Till well after the Reformation there were parishes where it was true that the parson was the 'person' of the parish because of his education.

The Reformation re-discovered the doctrine of the priesthood of all believers, but ministers in reformed churches became almost as dominant over their congregations as their Roman predecessors had been. Docility of the laity had become a thousand year old habit and it needed more than a Reformation to shake it. Further, the Reformed emphasis on preaching brought reformation churches under the power of the preacher as their predecessors had been under the power of the priest. Lutheran and Calvinist churches and their off-shoots have always been most careful in their standard of ministry. This is good, but the division from the laity again

71

became emphasized. (This was accentuated by the fact that new churches could not be organized without the help of princes and political leaders. The godly prince and the minister had such a place in Church matters that there was little room for others. Calvin's presbyterian form of government brought in the laity but even then the minister remained the real leader.)

For four centuries, with some notable exceptions, the laity have been content to let the clergy run the Church and give what help they can to the parson in the spare time, their job and their home allow them. Today the clergy are short-handed and there is much talk about 'using our laity,' and all sorts of schemes are being propounded to help clergy to run the parochial machine more effectively, but is this what the New Testament has in mind when it speaks about the *laos?* Speaking to a conference of clergy Hans Ruedi-Weber, Secretary of W.C.C. Dept. on the Laity said :

'What we are interested in is not what the laity should do for the Church, but how the laity can be the Church in the world. The laity are not helpers of the clergy, so that the clergy can do this job: but clergy are helpers of the whole people of God, so that the laity can be the Church.'

This point was made at Evanston and reiterated at New Delhi. In the section on Witness in the preliminary report entitled *New Delhi Speaks*, there is this passage :

'The pastor and the layman must learn to work as a team, each recognizing that the other has an essential ministry and gift of grace for his own special task in the one Body of Christ. There is an urgent need for all church members to recover the true meaning of certain words : to learn that the laity is really the *Laos*, that is, the whole people of God in the world, including, of course, those who have been ordained; to learn that ministry means any kind of service by which a Christian, exercising his particular skill and gift, however humble, helps his fellow-Christians or his fellow-men in the name of Christ. A far richer fellowship and team-spirit is bound to appear as soon as the whole Church comes to realize its function as the People of God, which God himself has provided with many kinds of ministry, in which one special kind of ministry, that of the ordained clergy, is set apart to strengthen and teach, to encourage and unite all the several witnesses in their various callings whose ministry is set in the heart of the secular world's manifold activity'[4] (*New Delhi Speaks*, p. 26).

Lambeth was saying the same when it declared: 'Baptism and confirmation constitute "the ordination of the laity" for the task of evangelism'[5] (p. 75).

It may help us to evaluate lay spirituality today if we examine it in the not too distant Anglican past; in the Evangelical and Oxford Revivals. All of us Anglicans are, to a greater or lesser extent, whether we like it or not, heirs of both these great movements. The heart of Evangelical piety was the Christian home, and in the Christian home, lay and clerical alike, the practice of family prayers. G. W. E. Russell gives this not altogether sympathetic picture of family prayers in his own home in mid-Victorian England (nor must it be regarded as altogether typical):

'We had family prayers twice every day. My father read a chapter, very much as his fancy took him, or where the Bible opened of itself; and he read without note or comment. I remember a very distinct impression on my infant mind that the portions of the Bible which were read at prayers had no meaning, and that the public reading of the words without reference to sense, was an act of piety. After the chapter, my father read one of "Thornton's Family Prayers," and indeed the use of that book was a distinctive sign of true Evangelicalism. Some friends of ours tried extempore prayers, and one worthy baronet went so far as to invite contributions from the servants. As long as only the butler and the house-keeper voiced the aspirations of their fellows all was decorous; but one fine day an insubordinate kitchen-maid took up her parable saying, "And we pray for Sir Thomas and her Ladyship too. Oh may they have new hearts given to them!" The bare idea that there was room for such renovation caused a prompt return to the lively oracles of Henry Thornton'[6] (*Household of Faith*, p. 241).

How much Evangelical laity used the Book of Common Prayer in family or private prayers it is difficult to ascertain, but they believed in its careful and reverent use in church.

The practice of private Bible reading and private prayer was maintained by very early rising. Some of the Clapham Sect, for instance, kept time-tables to discipline themselves in this matter. Many Evangelicals kept a diary not for the purposes of keeping a chronicle but as a means of self-examination at the end of the day leading to thanksgiving and confession of sin. Principles of Christian stewardship can be seen in the character of Henry Thornton who gave away two-thirds of his income before his marriage. Henry Thornton was a member of the Clapham Sect and the author of the book of family prayers referred to by G. W. E. Russell. Evangelicals were strict in their attitude to what they called 'worldly amusements' and they became stricter as the nineteenth century progressed. They were on the whole vigorous Sabbath-keepers. Wilberforce wrote in his old age: 'Often on my visits to Holwood (Pitt's country home), when I heard one or another speak of this man's place or that man's peerage, I felt a rising inclination to follow the same objects, but a Sunday in solitude never failed to restore me to myself' (p. 187).[7] The pursuit of personal holiness as a gift from God was linked with a sense of moral accountancy to God for every action which gave many a sense of integrity which changed the moral climate of England.

Sir Robert Ensor in his final volume of the *Oxford History of England* says:

'The essentials of evangelicalism were three. First, its literal stress on the Bible. It made the English the "people of the book," somewhat as devout Moslems are, but as few other Europeans were. Secondly, its certainty about the existence of an after-life of rewards and punishments. If one asks how nineteenth-century English merchants earned the reputation of being the most honest in the world (a very real factor in the nineteenth-century primacy of English trade), the answer is: because hell and heaven seemed as certain to them as tomorrow's sunrise, and the Last Judgement as real as the week's balance-sheet. This keen sense of moral accountancy had also much to do with the success of self-government in the political sphere. Thirdly, its corollary that the present life is only important as a preparation for eternity. Exalted minds in abnormal moments may have reached that feeling in all ages, and among primitive peoples it has often moved mass enthusiasms. But the remarkable feature of evangelicalism was that it came so largely to dispense with the abnormal; made other-worldliness an everyday conviction and, so to say, a business proposition; and thus induced a highly civilized people to put pleasure in the background, and what it conceived to be duty in the foreground, to a quite exceptional degree.'[8]

A similar pursuit of holiness characterized the Oxford Movement, whose importance Dr. Owen Chadwick says lies in its devotional rather than its doctrinal consequences. Methods and emphasis were of course different. Whereas the devout Evangelical layman received Holy Communion regularly once a month, his Tractarian brother communicated weekly and if possible more frequently. Instead of self-examination in the pages of a diary came confession in the presence of a priest. (The Evangelical view of confession was that there is no sin as bad as that of confessing it to a priest.) Evangelicals took great care in the taking of Church services. Tractarians added to this a loving care of the Church building to make it in every way worthy of the great God to whom worship was offered. One of the essential points in Tractarian teaching which Pusey made in 1840, was, 'Regard for the visible part of devotion, such as the decoration of the house of God, which acts insensibly on the mind.' [9] Other new features were the introduction of retreats and quiet days, which were made available to the laity, and later of the existence of members of the new Anglican religious orders who have contributed so much in the taking of such retreats. Here and elsewhere the laity have been made aware of methods of prayer stemming from the Counter-Reformation. Canon Charles Smyth pays this tribute to Tractarian piety in *The Church and the Nation*. He writes:

'The Tractarian influence persists among us to this very day, not only in such externals as ecclesiastical furnishings (never the strongest feature of the Movement) and in the conscious reverence with which Anglicans of the older generation have been taught to behave in church, but also in a type of character—disciplined, recollected, strong, serious and yet always cheerful though never flippant, quiet, reserved, unworldly, unassertive, and above all, grounded in the tradition of the Church of England and in the piety of the Book of Common Prayer; a type of character which is not seldom met with in priests and in the devout laity, both men and women, and of which Mr. Keble was himself a notable exemplar: an old-fashioned English Churchman, . . . with a frank, gay humility of soul . . . great unselfishness, strict and severe principles of morals and duty' [10] (Smyth, p. 173).

It might be said that whereas the Tractarians and their successors encouraged their laity to come regularly to the expert for

75

F

advice and absolution to enable them to live a holy life within a sacramental society, the Evangelicals encouraged their laity to leave behind their dependence on the pastor and as mature Christians to exercise their own priesthood with the guidance of the Holy Spirit. It is significant that the work of devotion which the Archdeacon of Auckland has chosen to represent the Evangelical Movement is by a layman, William Wilberforce.[11]

Both movements had their weak points. The Evangelical layman tended to be far too individualistic in his piety. Evangelicals as a whole had not grasped the biblical doctrine of the Church as the visible Body of Christ of which all the baptized are members. This, on the other hand, was the strength of the Oxford Movement; but here, although there was this emphasis on the corporateness of the Church as a divine visible institution, piety tended to be almost as individualistic as Evangelical piety. The laity were taught 'to make their communions,' to come to a quiet service in the early morning to receive the sacrament, and to a later service for worship. The distinction between clergy and laity was greatly increased by the Oxford Movement and it was almost true that the Church was thought of as a society of the clergy plus the laity.

However it was Bishop Gore who wrote in *Essays in aid of the Reform of the Church:* 'The two permanent obstacles to the restoration of the laity to their original position in the Church are the clerical love of exclusive control and the widely diffused and deeply ingrained lay apathy.' [12] Many Tractarians had little interest in the world outside the Church. Von Hügel strongly criticized Pusey as being 'uncatholic' because he seemed incapable of taking any interest in anything that was not technically religious, or that was not explicitly connected with religion.

Further the very wholesome stress on the necessity of beauty and dignity in church buildings and worship has contributed to the not so wholesome belief amongst the laity today that what happens on church premises is 'religious' and what happens elsewhere is not. There have been many protests against this. Bishop Gore comes to mind as well as William Temple, but there is nevertheless a 'churchiness' about much of our lay spirituality today which might not have been so pronounced if there had been no Oxford Movement. In the writings of John Venn and Charles

Simeon I have found the opposite emphasis, presumably because they were facing the same problem. Venn asks: 'How many imperious masters, idle servants, unkind husbands, undutiful children, and unfaithful friends are zealous in their prayers, in attendance upon preaching, in reading the Scriptures, and in religious discourse, without perhaps a doubt of the genuine nature of the religion in which they confide?' [13] Or again: 'Religion is not merely an act of homage paid on bended knees to God; it is not confined to the closet and the church, nor is it restrained to the hours of the sabbath; it is a general principle extending to man's whole conduct in every transaction and in every place' [14] Simeon too made the same practical demands of his people and of himself. Here is his own account of a meditation on 1 Corinthians 13:

'When reading 1 Corinthians 13 this morning I asked myself "How should I act towards Mr. and Mrs. Edwards and Mr. and Mrs. Thomason?" and regretted that the same spirit did not animate me towards every other person. I began to pray for our Provost, and Mr. Flower, and Mr. Twiss, the grocer. I apprehend that the best mode of understanding the nature and extent of Christian love is to consider what dispositions we show towards the dearest objects of our affections, and to put every human being in their place.' [15]

II. LAY SPIRITUALITY TODAY

There are certain things to be borne in mind:

1. The division between sacred and secular remains a false division: what is true and right in church on Sundays is also right and true at the office and or on the shop-floor on Mondays.

2. The difference between clergy and laity is one of function within the total priesthood of the Church; it is not one of status. We need to follow the New Testament and New Delhi in seeing clergy and laity as an equal partnership. The great change that has come in our own day in the relationship between parson and people is educational. The layman is not only better educated than he has ever been before; in many parishes it is the clergy who get most easily out of their depth intellectually.

3. The spirituality of the last 200 years has, as we have seen,

been primarily pietistic and individualistic. The question we need to ask is: 'Do we need a more corporate lay spirituality than either the Catholic or Evangelical traditions have yet supplied?'

4. The pressures of the modern world will make the pattern of lay spirituality today different from what they have been in former ages.

In the modern world lay Christians seem to make one of two mistakes. The first is that they become so identified with the world from Monday to Saturday that there seems little difference in their way of life or moral judgments from the man working at the next bench or the woman next to be served in the shop. The second is that they become so separate from their neighbours at work or in the community at home, that they get the reputation of being 'Bible-punchers,' and the only group in which they have any influence is the 'holy huddle' of the already converted whom they gather round themselves. This may be a caricature, but it is true enough to suggest the ineffectiveness of much of our lay spirituality today. On the one hand the layman needs to see that the whole of his life is the subject of his prayers and dedication to Christ. On the other hand he needs to watch any tendency to make his bench or office-desk a pulpit for getting at his colleagues. If he does so he will become isolated and insulated from the rest of the community in which he works.

A more positive attitude than either is to be found in what the Prior of Taizé has to say about the Christian attitude to the present cult of sexual licence among young people:

'In the climate in which we live in the West it would be easy to adopt a puritanical attitude and seek to build up in Christian circles an uneasy conscience about the life of the senses. The school-master outlook which in the past has succeeded with childish mentalities today runs the risk of having the opposite result. Any narrowness, any over-ready judgment will result in separating us irredeemably from the younger generation. The only way is to stay completely humane. We are this when we know how to help the man next to us to rediscover by his own efforts moral concepts that he will be able to put into practice without any pressure from outside.

'Our way of being present in the world will, moreover, be more convincing than talk . . .'[16]

This is surely true of a wider area that he is considering, it points to that 'holy worldliness' of which Dr. Vidler writes. In this attitude the separation from the world is an inner detachment and the note of criticism may be there, but it is not explicit. At a meeting between St. Aidan's College students and a Christian Trade Union group at Wigan the question was asked: 'What difference does it make to you to be a Christian at work?' The answer from one came back: 'People take no notice of me most of the time, but when they are in trouble it is to me that they come.' Here is surely the key, here is a Christian priesthood being exercised on the level of reality and helpfulness, here is a dedicated life through which Christ shines.

But we clergy do not give as much help as we might to our laity because we do not enable them to live on the level of reality. It may be that we do not fully understand that the difference between clergy and laity is not merely one of function within the Body of Christ, but of occupation 'as we have it in the Census returns.' That last phrase comes from an article by W. G. Symons in *Frontier*. He goes on:

'A minister is concerned in his daily work with "religion" in the specific sense; he is involved with "secular affairs," either in his spare time, or in ways which have to be consciously related to the religious duties and causes which he has accepted as his life's work. In contrast the layman is engaged during his working hours in a "secular" occupation, and his religious activities must be limited to his spare time (however much his faith may inform and enlighten what he does at work). One simple manifestation of this different situation is that the minister, in the nature of things, shares a common faith with his professional colleagues, whereas an ordinary layman lives in a mixed working community of believers and unbelievers. These differences produce a subtle but profound difference of outlook or "perspective." Clerical exhortations often seem, to lay minds, to identify "the service of God" with those aspects of life which are the professional concern of the clergy (or, as Dr. Spurgeon put it more shortly, "ministers will *parsonificate* the Gospel").' [17]

We also need to think more carefully about the sense of unreality the ordering of our services may convey to the laity. Take, for instance, the Vesper hymn at Evensong. Are we really justi-

79

fied in singing at 7.45 p.m. 'The day thou gavest Lord is ended' or 'Now the day is over' when we know very well that most of our congregation are going home not just to supper and bed, but to 'Sunday Night at the Palladium' and 'Armchair Theatre' and that for them it will be somewhere between eleven and midnight before their day is either over or ended? [18]

A sense of reality and of its corporate nature needs to be brought also into our Communion services. The Eucharist is not something done by the priest for the people, it is something priest and people do together. There are some welcome signs of change in this direction—the use of the westward position, the substitution of loaves of bread for wafers, the introduction of an offertory procession, and a general increase in those parts of the service in which the laity can join, like the Prayer of Humble Access.

If we are going to answer the question about a more corporate lay spirituality we must look at family religion. Grace before meals is surely a practice for all Christians in all ages. Family prayers are far more difficult to organize than a hundred years ago, with father and perhaps mother out to work and the children having their breakfast at different times because of going to different schools. It may be possible to have family prayers once a week, perhaps at week-ends. In some homes where the mother does not go out to work and the children leave for school about the same time, it is possible for brief family prayers at the breakfast table.

The rediscovery of the 'House Church' is perhaps the most significant development in our time in family worship. Instead of the mid-week celebrations being taken in church they are mostly held in a number of different homes in the parish and are attended by members of the family and friends. Such services take place early morning or early evening. On a college visit to Halton two years ago, I had direct experience of this. A group of any number up to a dozen sit on chairs round a small table in the living room. The hostess provides the bread, a table cloth and a jug of water for the ablutions. The celebrant asks one person present to read the Epistle, another the Gospel and a third the Comfortable Words. There is always a brief sermon and an opportunity for open prayer before the Prayer for the Church Militant. When the service is over, a sort of Agape follows consisting of tea and bread and butter or a bun. The group stays chatting for a time, while those leave who have to catch early buses for work. (In no other parish have I found the laity so readily able to talk naturally about their faith in Christ.) Other parishes have followed Halton's example but they are fewer than might be expected. There is, however, a growing practice of house services and home meetings (in fact there was a description of house services in a Swindon parish in *Church and People* (1962), the journal of the C.P.A.S.). Such meetings and services are usually evangelistic, but is there any reason why the same pattern might not be adopted for instruction of Christians by means of Bible and discussion groups? A strong corporate spirituality may well be encouraged by a move away from the church, the hall, the school and from even the vicarage into the homes of the people themselves.

Though there is no substitute for private Bible study and private prayer, some interesting experiments in corporate Bible study have reached this country since the war. They have been used in Bible Weeks and information about them is available in booklets by Edwin Robertson and Harold Wilson. One such method is known as the 'Swedish Method.' A carefully selected and not too long passage is taken, for example a parable or a portion of an epistle and read either by the group leader or in silence. The members first is a question mark, the second an arrow and the third a are given a post-card divided into three equal spaces. Against the candle. The group is given a set period of say a quarter of an hour to work at the passage themselves. In the question column he puts anything he does not understand, or does not agree with; in the second anything that needs to be acted upon, and in the third column any new light that comes to him from the passage. The leader asks each to read his findings and general discussion follows. The third column can also be used for new thoughts that emerge out of the group discussion.

Finally we have to consider the most difficult problem of all— that of private Bible study and prayer. Here it is for me to pose the questions and for others to supply the answers. How many, do you think, of the laity who take Bible Reading Fellowship or Scripture Union notes use them regularly? What sort of prayers do lay people use out of church, and under what conditions do they use them? Is God for many churchpeople like the doctor or the plumber, someone to be called in, in an emergency, with the hope that he will not be required again? I take it that most Christian people pray when they are facing a crisis like an operation or a bereavement or a change of work; but what about other times? Do they get further than their childhood prayers of 'God bless Mummy and Daddy and Aunt Jane'? How many people use books of prayers or even have their Bible and Prayer Book out for use in the home? How many who want to pray are seriously hindered by noise and distraction and not having a room of their own? Are people prepared to grow in prayer?

An attempt to answer this sort of question has been made by John Townroe, Warden of Warminster, in two articles published in *Theology*, entitled 'Prayer for Busy People' and 'No Time for Prayer.[19] He quotes a priest who said 'all the spiritual books seem to be written for people with servants'—he might have added that they were written for people free from family ties, i.e. monks and bachelor parsons, for the needs of the family man and mother with young children are seldom considered. Mr. Townroe also most helpfully lists 'features of our time which make special diffi- culties for a life of prayer.' These are:

  lack of privacy (through rise of population and over- crowding);
  noise (invading town and country alike);
  rush (as distinct from sheer speed);
  activism (as distinct from purposeful activity);
  over-strain (proceeding ultimately from a lack of faith);
  and a certain kind of nervous restlessness which is all- pervading.

To these he added in the second article:

  distraction (caused by the increase of inviting and enter- taining diversions);
  undue pressure (resulting from the cult of efficiency carried to extremes);
  tension (induced by high-pressure commercialism, and the 'go-getting' of the West).

His articles deal realistically with the two problems of 'what' and 'when.' What sort of prayer should be commended to the laity, and when might they find time to pray? To the question what, Mr. Townroe recommends the prayer of contemplation. He may be right but there are many of us who do not approach our prayers that way round. However, as a larger proportion of the laity are better educated than their forefathers they can be ex- pected to be more intelligent in their praying. This *may* mean that some will be capable of contemplation; it will certainly mean that more Christians could make room for mental prayer, usually with the Bible open. However I should also have thought that with care and planning the traditional pattern of adoration, thanksgiving, confession, petition, intercession and dedication can still be used even if the various parts of the pattern have to be spread over several days. A helpful approach is to be found in Bishop Robert Nelson's *The End of a Golden String,* which not only deals practically with the modern world but sets out a scheme of intercessions for a week, morning and evening. His plan is followed in the excellent C.M.S. handbook *Take Your Time.* There is also much to help the layman in seven sermons on Prayer which Dr. Vidler has included in his *Windsor Sermons.*

Morning and Evening Prayer for the layman may not be entirely realistic. Many people work, or go to school at a distance, having to get up very early. The average mother with small children finds that silence ends as soon as the first child wakes. For many lay people some time in the early evening may well be best. Of course for those who work in big cities there are usually churches open which can be visited in the lunch-hour, offering quiet and perhaps a Bible and a Prayer Book as well. Mr. Townroe answers the question 'when' by suggesting that though a layman may find it impossible to come by half an hour's solitude and silence each day, such times can be planned once or twice a week. It is true of course that a person who does have a time of quiet regularly, even if the intervals between are long, can use more fleeting opportunities, like travelling in a bus or train, or waiting for an appointment, for recollection and arrow prayers. No less than the clergy, the laity should be encouraged to make an annual retreat or at least a Quiet Day for restoration of vision and renewal.

Here I end. There might well be some further questions on whether there is room for more asceticism today in the questions of food, drink, tobacco and sleep. But these are problems that are the concern of the clergy as much as the laity. The chief thing we clergy need to do is to realize that the day of the layman has come; that he is neither a child nor an adolescent but a growing man. We should treat him as such and encourage him to seek an adult spirituality within the corporate life of the Church.

NOTES

[1] F. R. Barry, *Asking the Right Questions* (1960), pp. 87–8.
[2] A. R. Vidler, *Windsor Sermons* (1958), XXI.
[3] T. M. Lindsay, *Church and Ministry in the Early Centuries* (1903), footnote pp. 245–6.
[4] *New Delhi Speaks* (1962), p. 26.
[5] *The Lambeth Conference, 1958*, 2, p. 75.
[6] G. W. E. Russell, *The Household of Faith* (1906), p. 241.
[7] R. Coupland, *Wilberforce* (1945), p. 187.
[8] R. C. K. Ensor, *England 1870–1914* (1936), pp. 137–8.
[9] C. H. Smyth, *The Church and the Nation* (1962), p. 169.
[10] ibid., p. 173.
[11] C. J. Stranks, *Anglican Devotion* (1961), Chapter 8.
[12] C. Gore, *Essays in aid of the Reform of the Church* (1898), p. 16.
[13] M. M. Hennell, *John Venn and the Clapham Sect* (1958), p. 206.
[14] ibid., p. 205.
[15] W. Carus, *Memoirs of the Life of the Rev. Charles Simeon, M.A.* (1847), p. 219.
[16] R. Schutz, *This Day Belongs to God* (1961), p. 25.
[17] W. G. Symons, 'The Things that are Secular' in *Frontier*, Autumn 1962, p. 509.
[18] I owe this point to the Reverend Eric Lord of Homerton College, Cambridge.
[19] J. Townroe in *Theology*, July 1955 and December 1959. The former is reprinted by S.P.C.K. as a pamphlet.

THE EVANGELICAL DOCTRINE OF BAPTISM

by

J. R. W. STOTT

THE EVANGELICAL DOCTRINE OF
BAPTISM

LET me introduce this subject with two preliminary statements:

(i) *Evangelical churchmen do not treat the sacrament of baptism lightly.* We do not forget that it was instituted by the risen Lord, nor that it was administered by the infant Church from the Day of Pentecost onwards (Acts 2:38, 41). Because of the precept of Christ and the practice of the apostles, it is the plain duty of every professing Christian to ask for baptism for himself and his children; and of the ordained minister to press upon his congregation this obligation and privilege.

(ii) It is the claim of the evangelical churchman that his doctrine of baptism is *the biblical doctrine.* At all events, he could not contemplate the existence of an *evangelical* doctrine of baptism as distinct from a *biblical* doctrine; since his primary concern is to understand the biblical doctrine and to conform his thinking and practice to it. If the so-called 'evangelical' doctrine of baptism can be shown to be unbiblical, the evangelical churchman is ready to abandon it in favour of any doctrine which can be shown to be more biblical.

My task then is first to seek to establish the biblical doctrine of baptism, and secondly, to show that the teaching of the Book of Common Prayer and the Articles can and should be interpreted in a way that is fully consistent with the biblical doctrine.

In this study I am *not* concerned with the proper *mode* of baptism (whether by affusion or immersion), nor with the proper *subjects* for baptism (whether adults and infants, or adults only); but rather with the meaning and the effect of the sacrament, that is, what it signifies and how it operates.

I. THE MEANING OF BAPTISM

The best way to introduce the meaning of baptism is to assert that both the sacraments of the gospel are essentially sacraments of *grace,* that is, sacraments of divine initiative, not of human activity. The clearest evidence of this in the case of baptism is that, in the New Testament, the candidate never baptizes himself, but always submits to being baptized by another. In his baptism, he is a passive recipient of something that is done to him. The

Articles are quite clear about this. For instance, Articles 25, 27 and 28 all begin with the statement that a sacrament is a sign not of what we do or are, but of what God has done, or does.

Now, granted that baptism is a sacrament of grace, what grace of God does it signify? The answer to this question is threefold.

(a) *Baptism signifies union with Christ.* God's chief grace to undeserving sinners is his plan to unite them to his Son. That this is the primary meaning of baptism is clear from the use of the preposition *eis* with the verb 'to baptize.' Just as the passage of the Red Sea was a baptism *eis* (into) Moses (1 Cor. 10:2), so Christian baptism is baptism not into any man (1 Cor. 1:13) but into Christ (Rom. 6:3). It is true that sometimes baptism is said to be *en* or *epi* the name of Christ (Acts 10:48, 2:38), but the commonest preposition is *eis*, 'into the Name of the Lord Jesus' (Acts 8:16, 19:5).

It is true again that, according to the Matthaean record of the institution of baptism, baptism was to be into the one Name of the three Persons of the Trinity (Matt. 28:19), but this gives place in Acts and the Epistles to baptism into the Name of Jesus —probably because it is he who revealed the Father and sent the Holy Spirit, so that we cannot be related to him without being related to them also.

Further, baptism into the Name of Christ is baptism into Christ crucified and risen (Rom. 6:3, 4). This union with Christ crucified and risen signifies participation in the virtue of his death and the power of his resurrection, the end (by death or burial) of the old life of sin, and the beginning (by resurrection or rebirth) of the new life of righteousness. This union with Christ in his death and resurrection, and the beginning of a new life, is the controlling idea in baptism, and the next two meanings simply amplify the benefit of sharing in the death and resurrection of Christ.

(b) *Baptism signifies the forgiveness of sins.* It is safe to say that all religious water rituals are purification ceremonies, and Christian baptism is no exception. 'Repent and be baptized every one of you in the name of Jesus Christ for the forgiveness of your sins,' said Peter on the Day of Pentecost (Acts 2:38, RSV). 'Rise, and be baptized, and wash away your sins, calling on his Name,' said Ananias to Paul (Acts 22:16, RSV). Similarly, it is

almost certain that the phrases 'but you were washed' (1 Cor.
6:11), and 'the washing of regeneration' (Titus 3:5) are refer-
ences to baptism. The washing of our bodies with pure water
(Heb. 10:22) signifies the washing of the soul from the defile-
ment of sin.

(c) *Baptism signifies the gift of the Spirit.* It is well known
that John the Baptist (according to the four evangelists) contrasted
his own water-baptism with the Spirit-baptism which the Messiah
would administer: 'I baptize you with water. . . . He will baptize you with the Holy Spirit' (Matt. 3:11). In view of this contrast, we would expect that when Jesus Christ began to baptize
with the Spirit, all baptism with water would cease. The fact that
water-baptism continued, by special command of the risen Christ,
suggests that it is now intended to signify the very Spirit-baptism
with which it had previously been contrasted. The pouring of
water by which we receive the baptism of water, dramatizes the
outpouring of the Spirit by which we receive the baptism of the
Spirit. Peter seems to have understood this on the Day of Pentecost, for, having interpreted the coming of the Spirit as the fulfilment of God's promise to pour out his Spirit on all flesh, he
said: 'Repent and be baptized every one of you in the name of
Jesus Christ for the forgiveness of your sins; and you shall receive
the gift of the Holy Spirit. For the promise is to you and to your
children and to all that are far off, every one whom the Lord our
God calls to him' (Acts 2:38, 39 RSV). Here baptism is associated with both the forgiveness of sins and the gift of the Spirit.

These two blessings were distinctive blessings of the New
Covenant promised by God through the prophets. Baptism is
therefore to be understood as an eschatological sacrament, inas-
much as it initiates into the New Covenant which belongs to the
New Age. It does this by incorporating us *into Christ,* for Jesus
Christ is the mediator of the New Covenant, and the bestower of
its blessings.

To sum up, baptism signifies union with Jesus Christ in his
death and resurrection, involving the end of the old life (through
the forgiveness of sins) and the beginning of a new life (through
the gift of the Spirit). Alternatively, baptism signifies union with
Christ bringing both justification (a once for all cleansing and
acceptance) and regeneration (a new birth by the Spirit unto a
life of righteousness).

To these three meanings of baptism we must add that incorporation into Christ includes incorporation into the Body of Christ, the Church.

With all this the Book of Common Prayer is fully consistent.

(i) *Union with Christ.* In the Catechism, the second answer declares that in baptism 'I was made a member of Christ.' This is the controlling idea—incorporation into Christ. Such a union with Christ involves 'a death unto sin and a new birth unto righteousness' through becoming partakers of Christ's death and resurrection.

(ii) *Forgiveness.* Familiar expressions in the Baptism Service are 'the everlasting benediction of thy heavenly washing,' and 'the mystical washing away of sin.'

(iii) *The Gift of the Spirit.* 'Regeneration by thy Holy Spirit' is the gift signified in baptism for which we give thanks.

These two blessings are brought together in Article 27: 'the promises of the forgiveness of sins and of our adoption to be the sons of God by the Holy Ghost are visibly signed and sealed.'

(iv) *Church membership.* The service speaks of a reception, grafting, or incorporation into Christ's holy Church, or the congregation of Christ's flock.

We turn now from the meaning of baptism to its effect; from what it signifies to how it operates.

2. THE EFFECT OF BAPTISM

We would all (I imagine) agree with the definition of a Sacrament given in the Catechism: 'an outward and visible sign of an inward and spiritual grace given unto us, as a means whereby we receive the same, and a pledge to assure us thereof.'

So far we have been seeking to define the inward and spiritual grace of which baptism is the outward and visible sign. We now go on to define the relation between the visible sacrament and the invisible grace, between the sign and the thing signified, and thus to define the effect or operation of the sacrament.

Three main views have been held. The first is the view that the sign always conveys the gift, automatically, by itself, *ex opere operato,* so that all those who receive the sign willy nilly also receive the thing signified.

The second is the view (at the opposite extreme) that the sign effects precisely nothing. It *signifies* the gift visibly, but in no sense or circumstance *conveys* it. It is a bare token or symbol, and that is all. Neither of these is the evangelical doctrine of baptism.

The third and evangelical view is that the sign not only signifies the gift, but seals or pledges it, and pledges it in such a way as to convey not indeed the gift itself, but a title to the gift—the baptized person receiving the gift (thus pledged to him) *by faith*, which may be before, during or after the administration of the sacrament.

The best way to proceed will be to examine these three views consecutively—the *ex opere operato* view, the bare token view, and the covenant sign view.

(i) *The* ex opere operato *view.* This is the view that the sign always, inevitably and unconditionally conveys the thing signified, through the power of the sacrament itself, or of God's promise attached to the sacrament. The consequence of this view is to suppose that all baptized persons (especially infants) are regenerate.

Apart from the *pragmatic* argument that all baptized persons do not *seem* to be regenerate, for they do not supply evidence of their regeneration in a life of godliness and holiness, there are two strong *biblical arguments* against this view. They concern the nature of the Church, and the way of salvation.

(a) *The nature of the Church.* However unfashionable it may be today, the Bible does envisage a difference between the visible and the invisible Church. We do not mean by this that a person can belong to the invisible Church without responsible membership of a local, visible manifestation of it, but rather that it is possible to belong to a visible church without belonging to the true Church, the Body of Christ, which is invisible in the sense that its members are known to God alone (2 Tim. 2:19).

As St. Augustine wrote: 'Many of those within are without; and some of those without are within.' Again, Bishop John Pearson, in his famous *An Exposition of the Creed* wrote: 'I conclude therefore, as the ancient Catholicks did against the Donatists, that within the Church, in the public profession and external communion thereof, are contained persons truly good and sanctified, and hereafter saved, and together with them other persons void of all saving grace, and hereafter to be damned.'

91

G

Thus, St. John writes of certain heretics that 'they went out from us, but they were not of us . . . ' (1 John 2 : 19). They were members (doubtless baptized members), but though 'with us' outwardly and visibly, they were not 'of us,' not genuine, but spurious.

Similarly, Paul writes at the beginning of 1 Cor. 10 of the Old Testament Church in the wilderness 'that our fathers were all . . . baptized into Moses in the cloud and in the sea, and all ate the same supernatural food and all drank the same supernatural drink. . . . Nevertheless with most of them God was not pleased; for they were overthrown in the wilderness.' The apostle deliberately describes them as baptized communicants, who nevertheless were overthrown in the wilderness; which shows that baptized communicant membership of the church is no guarantee of salvation.

The significance of this distinction between the visible and the invisible Church is that the visible Church consists of the baptized, while the invisible Church consists of the regenerate. Since the two companies are not identical, not all the baptized are regenerate.

Simon Magus is an example. He professed faith, was baptized, and no doubt passed as a church member, but Peter described him as being yet 'in the gall of bitterness and in the bond of iniquity,' with his 'heart not right in the sight of God' (Acts 8 : 13–24).

If Paul could write 'he is not a real Jew who is one outwardly, nor is true circumcision something external and physical. He is a Jew who is one inwardly, and real circumcision is a matter of the heart, spiritual and not literal,' we could say the same of the Christian and baptism (Rom. 2 : 28, 29).

(b) *The way of salvation.* Salvation is variously described in the New Testament, but we have already seen that two of its constituent parts are Justification and Regeneration. One is a legal, the other a biological metaphor, but they are two sides of the same coin. It is impossible to be regenerate with being justified.

Over and over again the New Testament writers declare that we are justified by faith, or (more accurately) by grace through faith. It is impossible to reconcile this doctrine with the view that justification is by grace through baptism, with or without faith. If faith is necessary for salvation, then the unbelieving candidate is not saved through baptism. What Paul writes in Romans 6 about being baptized into Christ must not be interpreted in such a way that it contradicts his teaching in chapters 3 to 5 of the same epistle, that we are justified by faith.

Various attempts have been made to reconcile the doctrines of baptismal regeneration and justification by faith—mainly by diluting the meaning either of the regeneration of which baptism is the sacrament, or of the faith through which sinners are justified.

Thus, some of the schoolmen taught that if the necessary qualification for baptism in adults was repentance and faith, its equivalent in infants was simply their infantine condition; that is, the full-orbed saving faith of the New Testament was not necessary in their case.

Luther (followed by other reformers) attempted a reconciliation by asserting that God by his Word actually implants faith in infants to qualify them for baptism.

Others have tried to retain both baptismal regeneration and justification by faith by diluting the content not of faith but of regeneration. They debase it from the inward new birth unto righteousness (which it always means in the New Testament) into an admission to the external privileges of the Covenant; or into an implanted capacity or faculty which does not necessarily issue in good works, i.e. a goodness which is potential rather than actual; or into merely the negative remission of original sin (as Augustine, and some Calvinists). But there is no biblical warrant for this eviscerated idea of regeneration, which in Scripture always means a supernatural birth effected by the Holy Spirit and manifest in holy living.

These attempts to reconcile baptismal regeneration and justification by faith are unsuccessful because we have no right to give to either regeneration or faith any meaning less than their full biblical meaning. Therefore if a sinner is justified by God through faith alone, he is not regenerate through baptism without faith.

Turning to the Articles, we find their teaching consistent with the rejection of the *ex opere operato* view of baptism, namely their insistence that the efficacy of the sacraments is dependent on worthy reception. At the end of Article 25 there is the general statement that 'in such only as worthily receive the same they have a wholesome effect or operation . . .' Similarly, in Article 27, it is 'they that receive baptism *rightly*' who are grafted into the

Church, and to whom God's promises are visibly signed and sealed.

If we ask what is meant by a 'right' or 'worthy' reception, Article 28 explains 'insomuch that to such as rightly, worthily *and with faith* receive the same, the Bread which we break is a partaking of the Body of Christ . . . ' A right and worthy reception of the sacraments is a *believing* reception; without faith the sacraments have no wholesome operation or effect; rather the reverse.

The Catechism similarly lays emphasis on the necessary conditions required of candidates for baptism, and other statements in the Catechism which may be thought to support the *ex opere operato* view must be understood in the light of these conditions.

The benefits of baptism are not bestowed unconditionally; they are appropriated by faith. Unworthy reception brings not blessing but judgment.

To quote the Gorham Judgment: 'That baptism is a sacrament generally necessary to salvation, but that the grace of regeneration does not so necessarily accompany the act of baptism that regeneration invariably takes place in baptism; that the grace may be granted before, in, or after baptism; that baptism is an effectual sign of grace by which God works invisibly in us, but only in such as worthily receive it—in them alone it has a wholesome effect; and that without reference to the qualification of the recipient it is not in itself an effectual sign of grace; that infants baptized and dying before actual sin are undoubtedly saved, but that in no case is baptism unconditional.'

(ii) *The Bare Token view.* I think I can dismiss this view in a sentence or two. If baptism were a mere sign, which in no sense or circumstance whatever conveyed anything to its recipients, the apostles could never have used expressions which ascribe some effect to baptism like 'repent and be baptized for the remission of sins' (Acts 2 : 38), or 'as many of you as were baptized into Christ have put on Christ' (Gal. 3 : 27), or 'baptism now saves you' (1 Peter 3 : 21). In what sense these expressions should be interpreted we will discuss later; for the moment it is enough that they demolish the notion that baptism's function is merely to *signify* grace and not in any sense to *convey* it.

(iii) *The Covenant Sign view.* The evangelical (or 'reformed')

94

view of baptism is founded upon God's covenant of grace, and regards baptism as essentially the God-appointed sign which *seals* the blessings of the covenant to the individual Christian believer.

Pierre Marcel writes that 'the doctrine of the Covenant is the germ, the root, the pith of all revelation, and consequently of all theology; it is the clue to the whole history of redemption' (*The Biblical Doctrine of Infant Baptism,* p. 72).

Hooker wrote that 'baptism implieth a covenant or league between God and man' (*Ecclesiastical Polity,* V, lxiv, 4).

I cannot stop to argue that the so-called New Covenant (mediated by Jesus and ratified by his blood) was *new* only in relation to the Covenant of Sinai. In itself it was not New (as Paul argues in Galatians), but the fulfilment of God's covenant with Abraham, so that those who are Christ's are Abraham's seed, heirs according to promise (Gal. 3 : 29).

To quote Calvin, 'the covenant is the same, the reason for confirming it is the same. Only the mode of confirming is different; for to them it was confirmed by circumcision, which among us is succeeded by baptism.' [1] That is, baptism has replaced circumcision as the Covenant sign.

If this is so, and the place held by circumcision in the covenant in Abraham's day is occupied by baptism in the covenant in our day, what is this? The place and function of circumcision is defined in Rom. 4 : 11 (RSV), where Abraham is said to have 'received circumcision as a sign or seal of the righteousness which he had by faith while he was still uncircumcised.' Here it is said that Abraham received two gifts. First, he received justification, acceptance, by faith, while still uncircumcised. Secondly, he received circumcision as a sign and seal of this righteousness. The righteousness was given him in Genesis 15; its seal in Genesis 17. Now, what circumcision was to Abraham, Isaac and his descendants, baptism is to us. It is not only the sign of covenant membership, but a seal or pledge of covenant blessings. Baptism does not convey these blessings to us, but conveys to us a right or title to them, so that if and when we truly believe, we inherit the blessings to which baptism has entitled us.

But the receiving of the sign and seal, and the receiving of the blessings signified, are not necessarily (or even normally) simultaneous. To *truly believing adults* the covenant sign of baptism (like circumcision to Abraham when he was 99 years old) signifies and seals a grace which has already been received by faith. *To the infant seed* of believing parents, the covenant sign of baptism (like circumcision to Isaac at the age of 8 days) is administered because they are born into the covenant and are thereby 'holy' in status (1 Cor. 7 : 14), but it signifies and seals to them graces which they still need to receive later by faith.

This is the case also with *adults* who are baptized *in unbelief* and later believe. We do not rebaptize them. Their baptism conveyed to them a title to the blessings of the New Covenant; they have now claimed their inheritance by faith. This point was established in the early centuries of the Church in the case of the *fictus,* the person baptized in a state of unworthiness. He was not rebaptized, because a distinction was drawn between the title or *character* of baptism, which was always conferred on the recipient, and the *grace* of baptism, which depended on 'worthiness,' i.e. repentance and faith.

This accepted view regarding unqualified adults the Reformers applied from adults to infants. Again, the baptism of infants 'has a suspended grace accompanying it, which comes into operation upon their growing up and becoming qualified for it.' [2]

'Baptism, correctly administered, has thus one effect which is universal and invariable, whatever be the state or condition of the baptized person at the time, viz. a title or pledge for the grace of the sacrament upon worthiness.' [3]

'The grace of the sacrament is not tied to the time of its administration.' [4]

It is in this sense that the Articles refer to baptism as not only a sign of grace but a means of grace; and not only a sign, but an effectual sign of grace (Article 25), 'by the which God doth work invisibly in us, and doth not only quicken, but also strengthen and confirm our faith in him.' Since a sacrament is a visible word, and it is the function of God's word to arouse faith (Rom. 10 : 17), the sacraments stimulate our faith to lay hold of the blessings which they signify and to which they entitle us.

So the sacrament conveys the grace it signifies, not by a mechanical process but by conferring on us a title to it and by arousing within us the faith to embrace it.

'As baptism administered to those of years is not effectual unless they believe, so we can make no comfortable use of our baptism administered in our infancy until we believe. . . . All the promises of grace were in my baptism estated upon me, and sealed up unto me, on God's part; but then I come to have the profit and benefit of them when I come to understand what grant God, in baptism, hath sealed unto me, and actually to lay hold on it by faith.' So wrote Archbishop Ussher in his book *Body of Divinity*.

Similarly Jerome: 'They that receive not baptism with perfect faith, receive the water, but the Holy Ghost they receive not.'

But in neither sacrament is the gift tied to the time of the sacrament's administration. It is possible to receive the sign before the gift, as is usual in the case of infants, or to receive the sign after the gift, as is usual in the case of adults.

The question may be asked why, if baptism does not by itself confer the graces it signifies (but rather a title to them), the Bible and Prayer Book sometimes speak as if they did. I have already mentioned such phrases as 'baptized into Christ' (Rom. 6:3), 'as many as were baptized into Christ did put on Christ' (Gal. 3:27), 'baptism saves us' (1 Peter 3:21), and 'this child is regenerate' (Book of Common Prayer).

The answer is really quite simple. It is that neither the Bible nor the Prayer Book envisages the baptism of an unbeliever; they assume that the recipient is a true believer. And since 'baptism and faith are but the outside and the inside of the same thing' (James Denney), the blessings of the New Covenant are ascribed to baptism which really belong to faith (Gal. 3: 26, 28). Jesus had said 'he that believes and is baptized shall be saved,' implying that faith would precede baptism. So a profession of faith after hearing the gospel always preceded baptism in Acts. For instance, 'they that received the word were baptized' (2:41), 'they believed Philip preaching . . . and were baptized' (8:12), 'Lydia gave heed to what was said by Paul. And when she was baptized . . . ' (Acts 16:14, 15), 'believe on the Lord Jesus Christ, and thou shalt be saved . . . ' (16: 31–3).

It is the same in the Prayer Book service. There is no baptism in the Church of England except the baptism of a professing believer, adult or infant. The *adult* candidate's declaration of repentance, faith and surrender is followed by baptism and the declaration of regeneration. The same is true of an *infant* in the

1662 service, where it is not the godparents who speak for the child so much as the child who is represented as speaking through his sponsors. The child declares his or her repentance, faith and surrender, and desire for baptism. The child is then baptized and declared regenerate. So he is regenerate, in the same sense as he is a repentant believer in Jesus Christ, namely in the language of anticipatory faith or of sacraments.

It is in this sense too that we must understand the Catechism statement 'I was made a child of God.' It is sacramental language. I was 'made' a child of God in baptism, because baptism gave me a title to this privilege, not because baptism conferred this status on me irrespective of whether I believed or not.

J. B. Mozley writes of 'a class of statements which are literal in form, but hypothetical in meaning.' Again, he says it is 'a literal statement intended to be understood hypothetically' (p. 241).

CONCLUSION

Does it matter whether we teach that the sign and the gift, the sacrament and the grace, are always received simultaneously, or generally separately? Yes, it does matter. People need to be warned, for the good of their soul, that the reception of the sign, although it entitles them to the gift, does not confer the gift on them. They need to be taught the indispensable necessity of personal repentance and faith if they are to receive the thing signified. The importance of this may be seen in three spheres.

(a) *The doctrine of assurance.* There is a great danger in post-Christian society of people trusting in baptism itself for salvation, and thus having a false sense of security. It is true that baptism is intended to bring us assurance, but how? Not by the mere fact of its administration, but because as a visible word of God it signifies his promises and evokes our faith in them. True assurance depends on a worthy reception of baptism.

(b) *The discipline of baptism.* We are familiar with Bonhoeffer's castigation of the modern tendency to cheapen grace. 'The price we are having to pay today in the shape of the collapse of organized religion is only the inevitable consequence of our policy of making grace available at all too low a cost. We gave away the word and sacraments wholesale; we baptized, confirmed and absolved a whole nation without asking awkward questions, or insisting on strict conditions. Our humanitarian sentiment made us give that which was holy to the scornful and unbelieving. We poured forth unending streams of grace. But the call to follow Jesus was hardly ever heard. Where were those truths which impelled the early Church to institute the catechumenate, which enabled a strict watch to be kept over the frontier between the Church and the world, and afforded adequate protection for costly grace? . . . To baptize infants without bringing them up in the life of the Church is not only an abuse of the sacrament, it betokens a disgusting frivolity in dealing with the souls of the children themselves. For baptism can never be repeated.' [5]

And to quote from a sermon preached by the Rev. H. Hensley Henson [6] before the University of Oxford in 1896: 'The modern practice of unconditioned, indiscriminate baptizing is indecent in itself, discreditable to the Church and highly injurious to religion.'

Not that Scripture authorizes us to stand in judgment on the reality of people's profession. Prof. John Murray's distinction is that God reserves the right to admit people to the *invisible* Church, on their *exercise* of faith. He delegates to ministers the responsibility to admit to the *visible* church, on their *profession* of faith.

Some would say that it must be a *credible* profession, but then we begin to make arbitrary rules by which to assess credibility. Our task is to be faithful in teaching the *significance* of baptism and the *conditions* of its efficacy; and then not to baptize any but those who profess to be penitent believers, and their children.

(c) *The practice of evangelism.* The baptized may still need to be evangelized, that is, exhorted to repentance, faith and surrender, so as to enter into the blessings pledged to them in baptism. But if all the baptized are regenerate, we cannot evangelize them. We can treat them as backsliders and urge them to return, but we cannot summon them to come to Christ if they are already in Christ by baptism. Thus the *ex opere operato* view cuts the nerve of evangelism, and we are back where Whitefield found himself on his return from Georgia in 1738. He was eyed with suspicion by the bulk of the clergy as a fanatic. According to Bishop Ryle, 'They were especially scandalized by his preaching the doctrine of regeneration or the new birth, as a thing which many baptized persons greatly needed!'

THE ANGLICAN SYNTHESIS

NOTES

[1] Calvin, *Institutes* IV, xvi, 6.
[2] J. B. Mozley, *A Review of the Baptismal Controversy* (1862), pp. 48–9.
[3] Mozley, op. cit., pp. 40–1.
[4] Mozley, op. cit., p. 49.
[5] D. Bonhoeffer, *The Cost of Discipleship* (1957), pp. 47, 179.
[6] Bishop of Durham 1920–39.

THE FORGIVENESS OF SINS

by

J. L. HOULDEN

THE FORGIVENESS OF SINS

THE aim of this essay is to state—and to justify—a particular point of view on the subject of the forgiveness of sins, and then to outline areas of difficulty in current theory and practice in the Church of England in this connection. The method is to relate the teaching of the New Testament and the essential insights of the Faith to practical Christian life.

We begin at the simplest point—the oldest Christian creed of all; and as its first clause we find: 'Christ died for our sins according to the Scriptures (1 Cor. 15:3). Many other statements in the New Testament would corroborate this teaching with equal simplicity, and Gospel stories depict our Lord's power to forgive sins authoritatively even in the days of his flesh (e.g. Mark 2:1-12). They bear witness to the conviction that in some new and total way not hitherto possible, but wholly in accord with the foreshadowing of the Old Testament, the work—and especially the death—of Jesus had removed the sins of the world, or at least of those who accept him. This is a purely general statement and is satisfactory so far as it goes, but once we attempt to penetrate beyond the initial simplicity it immediately raises two problems; first, how are we to understand this new dispensation of forgiveness? How does it work? And second, even if we can establish its principles, how is it to be applied to the Christian in the continuing course of ordinary life? How, in other words, is the Church to deal with post-baptismal sin? We shall discuss these questions in turn.

I. HOW ARE WE TO UNDERSTAND THE NEW DISPENSATION OF GOD'S FORGIVENESS?

We shall briefly expound two great early Christian views of the matter—the Pauline and the Johannine—the two most articulate theologies in the New Testament.

St. Paul. First, a general point. It is a great mistake to treat Paul as if he were a systematic theologian. He wrote as occasion demanded, and a line of thought initiated in one place may be developed in an entirely different context. Moreover, he was a Jew, formed in an Old Testament culture. So he expresses his thought not in logical construction but by way of images, set side by side to illuminate the reader and form his mind. To appreciate his meaning best, we are to seek to absorb the message of his pictures by concentrating on them in turn. This point is often made, but more rarely acted upon, because our approach is so incurably philosophical, and we are inclined to build doctrine logically on the foundation of one or two of his images, while ignoring others.

What are the images which St. Paul uses to illuminate the forgiveness effected through Christ? Some are of more permanent value than others: some are almost wholly without practical usefulness now, except for those who take trouble to learn about the Jewish background which they presuppose.

(i) The quarrel made up: 2 Cor. 5:19. This is important because it *is* permanently useful. It is often neglected because of its simplicity, yet it is good to keep it in mind as a model because it makes most of the key points.

(ii) The freeing of slaves: Rom. 3:24; 1 Cor. 6:20. Jesus pays the price and man goes free from his bondage. (Note that it is neither stated nor implied who was the recipient of the price: it is not necessary to suppose that St. Paul had any recipient in mind. It is simply that God's act in Christ is the action which results in the liberation.)

(iii) The acquittal of the guilty: Rom. 5:1; Gal. 3:8 etc. This is more difficult than it looks at first sight, because of the difference in atmosphere and method between a western and an oriental court of law; the latter is assumed by St. Paul and the Old Testament language behind him. Briefly, the distinction is between a western conception of justice as abstract and static, and an eastern conception of justice in terms of dynamic action to set things right. The picture is not of an impassive judge deciding a case on its merits but of an active judge who intervenes to put things where they ought to be. In this case, the idea is that the guilty cannot earn their discharge, cannot merit the judge's acquitting act: it is a free act of his grace. In Christ, God, who is the judge, identifies himself with the accused and sets him free. The force of the image lies in the extraordinary generosity of God's act, topsy-turvy by all human notions of justice (Rom. 5:6–9).

Two technical points elucidate the image: first, the words 'justify,' 'justification,' 'righteousness' are all from the same root in Greek and the two quite separate words in English are apt to mislead. Second, we can illustrate the fact that God's righteousness betokens his positive action to set things in the 'right' place which he desires for them by noting that in the Old Testament God's righteous acts are things like the Exodus—bringing his people out of Egypt and into the Promised Land. It is a question of the execution of God's purpose and not of conformity to abstract moral norms.

(iv) The sacrifice offered: Rom. 3:25. The main difficulty lies in the word which is variously translated 'propitiation,' 'expiation' and (as an adjectival noun) 'mercy-seat.' In favour of 'propitiation' is the parallel use of a related word in 1 John 2:2 and a certain amount of evidence of reasonably contemporary Jewish thought along these lines (note the story of the seven Maccabaean martyrs in 2 Macc. 7, especially v. 38). Again, it tunes in with St. Paul's language in Rom. 1:18; 5:9 etc. about the wrath of God against man's sinfulness. The modern reader need not be accused of desiring a 'soft religion' if he finds it hard to take this to mean that our Lord's work was propitiatory in the full sense of (putting it crudely) 'calming down' God's anger, seen on the model of a man's anger. He will see this as, like the law court image, a Pauline paradox: God makes nonsense of our notions by acting with outrageous love to set us free. 'Stop hardening your hearts,' he is saying, 'and you will see that God's wrath is really love: he does not change, but you must.' The other criticism of the full or stark 'propitiation' theory is that it is at odds with the other Pauline images, in that while they stress the utter unity of the Father with the Son in whom he acts, this image tends to set the Son over against the Father: and yet St. Paul says that the Father sets forth the Son to be a propitiation—which some may see as not so much paradoxical as nonsensical: how can one provide the means for appeasing one's own wrath? Those who feel this will either translate 'expiation' or 'mercy-seat'—the place of the removal of sin in the Tabernacle, in the Book of Exodus, for which the word *hilastērion* commonly stands in the Greek Old Testament. Jesus is the means whereby sin is removed: either 'expiation' or 'mercy-seat' yields this sense.

(v) The triumph of the victorious leader: 2 Cor. 2:14. Christ leads us home to the Father like a conquering general leading his troops or his captives in procession, on returning from the wars.

(vi) The sons adopted: Rom. 8:14–16; Gal. 4:3–7. To be forgiven is to be received into adoptive sonship in the family of God in union with him who is the Son by nature. St. Paul uses this image in Rom. 8, and it is important to see that the next four chapters carry the idea of the society, into which the believer comes, two stages further: first in terms of Israel, the people of God (with the problems which that raised particularly for Paul the Jew in connection with Israel 'after the flesh'), then in terms of the image of the Body of Christ into which the believer is incorporated. So salvation is shown to be a matter which is corporate as soon as it is individual.

To sum up: St. Paul shows the divine grace as acting in Christ, one single saving purpose informing the work of Father and Son. In this work, the initiative is wholly God's, and its effect is to forgive man totally—quite contrary to his deserts, needing only his simple penitent reception of the gift—and to bring him into the free life of God's household. Divine forgiveness is not a separate act from divine acceptance, and both simply express the essence of divine being, which Christ manifests and lives out.

St. John. We left this Pauline image of the family to the last because it comes closest to St. John's approach, but the thought of the Fourth Gospel is much more 'stream-lined' than that of St. Paul. We shall make two points about it.

First, the whole Gospel is within the framework of the doctrine of Creation. Recently, it has become more and more clear that the Judaism of the first century A.D. was obsessed with the first two chapters of Genesis, because they seemed to contain, in cryptic form, the key to the understanding of two matters of enormous interest at that time: the structure of the universe and the plan of history. Many, varied and extravagant were the speculative systems derived from the meagre data of the Genesis Creation narrative, and among them stands John 1:1–14, sober and profound. Like Genesis, the Gospel begins 'in the beginning.' As God speaks words in order to carry out certain of his creative acts in Genesis, so in St. John we read, 'In the beginning was the Word . . .' As light and then living creatures are the results of God's creation, so in John 1:4, we have, 'In him was life; and the life was the light of men.' In Genesis 1:26–7, there is the creation of man, after God has spoken his word; in John 1:14, the word is made flesh

—the new Adam as the counterpart of the old (compare John 19:5, Pilate's words, 'Behold the man,' the Adam). The parallel between Genesis 1 and John 1:1–14 is close, but in the Gospel all the categories which are used (word, light, life) are identified with one another and ultimately with the Creator himself—because 'the Word was God.' They are also identified with Jesus who is the word-made-flesh: 9:5; 11:25. Adam was a being quite distinct from God, a creature of his hand: but Jesus is the living embodiment of God's whole purpose and mind, which is eternally, inexorably one.

If John 1:1–14 is a Genesis-inspired prologue, it may be that chapter 20 is an epilogue owing something to the same source, thus reinforcing the Creation frame of the Gospel. In Genesis 1:2 the spirit (= breath) of God moves over the waters and in Genesis 2:7 God breathes into man's nostrils and he comes to life. In John 20:22, Jesus breathes on his disciples (the verb is the same) and they receive the Holy Spirit—the breath of the new, eternal life (cf. John 3:6). In the garden of the Resurrection (20:15), Mary Magdalene, a second Eve, supposes Jesus to be the gardener, the rôle of the first Adam in Eden. So it might be, but even if this view of John 20 is ill-founded it does not affect the general point.

John sees the action of God in Christ as all of a piece with his eternal being and purpose. In our more simple-minded moments, we tend to think of Creation, Fall and Redemption as three quite separate phases in the drama. It is not so for St. John: what God meant by Creation, he always means. Redemption is simply his creative purpose pushing on in the face of human sin. It is not surprising that forgiveness is depicted in John 20:22–3 in Genesis language: to forgive is to create anew. So our Lord is seen against a backcloth not simply of his own times, nor even of Israel's history (as for example by St. Matthew), but of time and creation as a whole. The stress is on God's unfaltering life-giving purpose.

This leads on to the second point, which concerns St. John's way of expounding how God acted through Christ: how is creation furthered and life given? In other words, how is forgiveness brought about, expressed, applied?

Broadly, the Gospel falls into two parts (apart from the Passion Story): chapters 1–12 and 13–17, the Ministry and the Supper

H

Discourses. A comparison of the two parts yields this notable feature: that in the first, numerous statements are made about the relationship of Father and Son (expressing, in a variety of ways, their complete unity), while in the second, the statements are repeated but are extended to include the believer. Examples are: 10:30 and 17:11 etc., in terms of unity; 5:19f, 36 and 14:12, in terms of 'works'; 8:18 and 15:26f, in terms of bearing witness; 10:36 and 17:18, in terms of mission—the act of sending. Forgiveness or salvation 'work' by the mantle which covers both Father and Son being cast also over the believers. This doctrine comes near to that view of the new relationship with God which is expressed in 2 Peter 1:4 in terms of becoming 'partakers of the divine nature.' Clearly, this salvation is seen in a corporate sense: the group of disciples in the Upper Room in chapters 13 to 17 is representative of the Church as a whole in all ages. (In fact, many of the statements of the Lord in those chapters are applicable only, or mainly, to the post-resurrection Church.) So the creation of the Church as the redeemed community springs from the heart of the inner life of Father and Son. It is not a society external to that life: rather it results from the admission of men to share it. Point by point the characteristics of the divine life are extended to include those who believe. At the Last Supper this is established: the web is woven. And the cross enacts it. Man is remade, in Christ, in the image of God.

Both St. Paul and St. John express God's forgiveness in relational terms, but this is more true of St. John, and St. Paul's teaching also has a transactional quality (God doing something for man as well as God simply opening a sphere of life to man). In both writers, the forgiving act depends wholly on God's initiative and is established among us in the human nature of Jesus and by the perfection of his self-oblation to the Father. It is apprehended by man through total self-abandonment in response to this love, and is carried out by incorporation into the society of the forgiven, the Church, which lives solely in the life and power of the Lord—so much so that the vine (John 15) and the Body of Christ (Rom. 12; 1 Cor. 12) are appropriate images for it. To be forgiven is to enter the Church, the sphere of forgiveness or acceptance here in this world.

2. HOW IS THIS FORGIVENESS TO BE APPLIED TO
THE ORDINARY CHRISTIAN?

It is easy to see how this applies to our first entry into the sphere of grace; it is less easy to see how the permanent purpose of God is to apply to post-baptismal sin. The principles which we stated at the end of the last section still operate: but how is the Church to work them out? The first question which exercised the Church (and notice that it was clearly a question for the community not the individual to settle) was, how easily shall forgiveness be granted? In the earliest days, it was a question which caused much difficulty, as the varied answers given in the New Testament itself bear witness. The Epistle to the Hebrews (6:4) is evidence for a highly rigorist approach in some churches: if a man has once received forgiveness and entered the Christian community and then commits serious sin, clearly he must be excluded. The discussion in 1 John 5:16f. displays a more discriminating attitude: a distinction is made between degrees of sin. Matt. 18:21, and probably all the Gospel stories which show our Lord as the forgiver of sin (though they may refer only to the initial act), envisage a much more pastoral attitude, consistent with the patience and love of God. Similarly, though St. Paul recommends the exclusion of sinners and cannot be accused of indulgence (e.g., 1 Cor. 5:9ff.; 2 Thess. 3:6), it may be that ultimate reconciliation is in mind, even in the serious case of 1 Cor. 5:1-5, and 2 Thess. 3:15 mitigates the earlier severity. In the Shepherd of Hermas, 'one life' is allowed—another variation existing in the second century.

The virtue of the rigorist view is that it treats sin seriously and sees it as separating the sinner from God and so from the Christian community, his people. But it could not last: it fails to witness to the patient love of God for which the very act of the Incarnation is the evidence, and it fails to allow sufficiently for human frailty as distinct from sheer wickedness. In the end the policy of 'seventy times seven' won the day—clearly rightly as long as repentance is not made to appear superficial. The difficulty is that in the practical life of the Church that superficiality is hard to avoid.

An equally difficult problem is to preserve the New Testament insights on this matter both in the daily life of the Church and in the spirituality of the individual Christian. It is clear that in the first days just as Baptism incorporated a man into the Christian community, and the Eucharist expressed and maintained that incorporation, so sin involved separation from the community: it was an act not simply against God, but against 'God-in-his-Church'—by inference from the doctrine of the Church expressed in the images of the Vine and the Body of Christ (and others). To be in sin is to be excommunicate. Subsequent forgiveness therefore involved reconciliation with the Church: it was a matter for the community, to be carried out in due order. It was not a matter which concerned simply God and the individual. So in the early centuries penance and absolution were administered, with varying degrees of publicity, by the bishop. This approach seems to have all the marks of the essential elements of the Faith (see end of first section): it is incarnational, sacramental and ecclesiastical (which is a *good* word in the context of New Testament doctrine!). God is experienced in the life and activity of a community stemming from Christ, living on his resources and setting him forth.

But in the course of history, this approach has been exposed to three threats: individualism, legalism, and confusion with psychotherapy.

As the Church expanded, the exercise of penitential discipline within the congregation as a whole with the bishop as its normal ministerial representative was no longer possible. In the course of time and by a variety of ways, the normal procedure came to be that of confession and absolution with the priest filling the Church's role in the action, and authoritatively representing God-in-his-Church. It is not surprising that this method of repenting and receiving forgiveness came to be seen as serving primarily personal devotional ends, rather than as expressing the Christian's status before God within the Body. It became an item in a disciplined spiritual life, an act of piety, and no doubt most Anglicans who go to confession to a priest go for that motive—an ascetic rather than a theological one. (Notice that the remnants of its use in the Book of Common Prayer, in the Visitation of the Sick and the first exhortation in the Holy Communion, are wholly typical of the later Middle Ages in this respect if in no other, that they recommend it for the individual's personal spiritual benefit: there are no corporate implications, and there is of course no question of its being theologically integrated into the Christian scheme.)

Second, the danger of legalism. The Western Church has been particularly open to the danger of turning the penitential system into a legalistic machine, especially where serious, open sins are concerned. The whole apparatus of canon law and the ecclesiastical courts, with the quasi-spiritual appendage of indulgences, is sufficient evidence of this; bearing, as was almost inevitable in a large, international Church, the marks of a human legal system rather than of the pastoral care of Christ's flock. In the Church of England since the Reformation, this tendency has been curbed with reasonable success, for reasons good and bad. On the credit side, Anglican moral theology has always borne a marked pastoral stamp. But much of the reason for Anglican freedom from legalism lies in the sheer inefficiency of church courts from the reign of Elizabeth I, together with the unwillingnes of governments to encourage their effective jurisdiction.

The third threat to the proper Christian working of the forgiveness of sins in the Church is a more recent one. There is often a confusion between sin as moral action needing forgiveness and sin as weakness or even disease needing treatment. Clearly a given sinful act may have both characteristics, but that does not mean that the two approaches can easily—or even helpfully—be fused. Nor does it mean that a man should not be a priest unless he is qualified psychiatrically; still less that a priest should feel bound to act as if he were a psychiatrist whether he is qualified or not! This is not in the least to underestimate the significance of sin as sickness nor the necessity of its treatment from this point of view. But sin remains a moral matter between man and God, and the priest's role is that of representative of God-in-his-Church for the forgiving of sinners. Some of the common instinctive unwillingness to see sin as other than weakness to be cured lies in a sense that the other view depends upon a God who is primarily censorious. God is not eternally disapproving and waiting to pounce! He is wholly concerned to accept man: so first the moral matter must be set right—the relationship between God and man restored—and then God's healing, by whatever instrument, can follow.

The present position among Anglicans in this regard is disquieting. The Protestant 'godly discipline' disappeared long ago, and it seems unlikely that in the general decline of disciplined life the use of the confessional, so widely revived among Anglicans in the past century, is at present increasing. Nor can it be assumed that serious private self-examination and repentance are widespread even among the faithful. Certainly general confessions in church services lack depth and (by definition) particularity. It is all the more serious because this is a period when the frequency of Communion has increased on a great scale, and the whole connection of repentance and Communion has largely been lost. The sense that to be in serious sin is to be 'out of Communion' is rare.

Yet the 'Parish Communion movement' which has not avoided this unfortunate feature has certainly brought to many Anglicans a lively sense, theologically authentic, of what it means to live in the Body of Christ. So when we try to see remedies for the low ebb which the administration of the forgiveness of sins has reached, we are not discouraged from recommending the wider use of the confessional by a fear that it would be used in a purely individualistic way. Such an extension of its use seems to take account of the theological factors which we deemed necessary after investigating the New Testament evidence, and it has the advantage of building upon already existing foundations in Anglican practice. There must be few areas in which the notion is totally unfamiliar, even if it is widely disliked, for good reasons and bad. There seems no other way so likely to bring home to the individual his need of forgiveness by the Father in the Body of Christ our redeemer.

In this connection, the common Anglican formula about confession in the presence of a priest ('All may, some should, none must') is unfortunate: it eliminates its theological importance (stemming from the doctrine of the Body of Christ) and reduces it to a pastoral expedient—precisely the fault of late mediaeval piety.

It is difficult to see what can seriously be urged against it—unless we accept the infallibility of our own history—a concept difficult to reconcile with the continuing guidance of the Holy Spirit in the Church. Certainly the Protestant founding fathers were not opposed to it: Calvin and more particularly Luther were strongly in favour. Luther wrote of the practice of private confession to the priest: 'If a poor miserable beggar heard that in a certain place were being distributed rich alms of money and clothing, would he need to be taken there by a policeman? ... If you are poor and in misery, go and confess, and use this means to health. ... If, however, you despise this treasure, and if you are too proud to confess your sins, we conclude that you are no Christian, and that neither ought you to share in the Sacrament (of the Lord's Supper).' And again: 'So when I urge the practice of confession, I am but urging every man to be a Christian.' (See Thurian, *Confession*, p. 29.)

If it is objected that in this act the priest comes between the believer and God, it ought to be clear that he is no more falsely mediatorial than in any other of his activities (preaching, baptizing, advising etc.). Always he is the representative of God and the Christian community, a dual role. And if it be objected that the act is not specifically ordained in the Bible, it should be seen that the early Church clearly recognized a God-given authority to forgive sins (John 20:22f, etc.), and it is a question of finding the most effective way of exercising that authority in the present-day Church. We generally fail to exercise it at all in any deeply significant way. Penitence needs to be elicited, stirred and met in ways appropriate to our circumstances—both the permanent ones of our faith and the changing ones of our present condition—for the feeding of the flock with the loving forgiveness of the eternal Father.

Further reading:
R. C. Mortimer, *The Origins of Private Penance in the Western Church* (O.U.P.)
Fr. Hugh, s.s.f.: *No Escape from Love* (Faith Press)
Max Thurian: *Confession* (S.C.M.)
Martin Thornton, o.g.s.: *Christian Proficiency* (S.P.C.K.), especially chapter 9
John Livingstone: *A Layman's Rule* (Church Literature Association)

THE DOCTRINE OF THE CHURCH

by

LESLIE MINHINNICK

THE DOCTRINE OF THE CHURCH

'THE visible Church of Christ is a congregation of faithful men, in the which the pure Word of God is preached, and the Sacraments be duly ministered according to Christ's ordinance in all those things that of necessity are requisite to the same' (Article XIX, Of the Church).

Is this where the modern Christian is to start when he begins to set in order his thoughts about the Church? Or are the Thirty-Nine Articles of Religion merely dated documents of the controversies of the sixteenth century, irrelevant to the thoughts and discussions of our own day? Are the Articles merely the preserve of the theological student, puzzles to be investigated in the historical study of the Faith?

Is it an alternative to say that we must go back to some other, earlier, period of Christian history, when the issues appear simpler, and we are nearer the fountainhead of divine truth and inspiration? Are we to go back to the Church of the Early Fathers, and find there the kind of idea and organization which was successful in combating the might of the Roman Empire? Would the copying of the Church of an earlier pagan world help the Church of the twentieth century in dealing with a situation which is not without its parallels?

Or are the writings of the Early Fathers even further removed from the world of modern man than both the simplicities and profundities of the Gospels? It is not always easy to find theological inspiration in the writings of the second and third centuries.

Are we then to go to the Bible—and increasingly when people say 'the Bible' they mean the New Testament—and reconstruct from texts containing the word 'ecclesia' what is the biblical doctrine of the Church? Is it the case that there is to be found in the pages of the Christian writings of the first century a logical and precise 'doctrine of the Church' which is to be uncovered and then used to test the orthodoxy of Christian bodies? Or, when we look for 'doctrines' in the pages of Scripture, are we seeking to impose categories of thought upon material which is of a very different order? May it not be the case that there is an imprecision, a poetical and almost lyrical quality, about the books of the Bible, a reluctance on the part of writers to seek to explain in direct logical terms the thoughts which are theirs, so that they seek refuge in symbol and analogy?

In any case, are we committed in the middle of the twentieth century to working out a doctrine in the sense in which this was pursued by bygone generations? Do the words 'orthodox' and 'unorthodox,' 'heterodox' and 'heretical,' still have for us the meanings which they had for our forefathers, or are they antiquated words relating to strange and precise states of mind which would put a strait-jacket on the free expression of Christian truth and charity, and the free working of the Spirit of God?

It is doubtful whether we have yet accepted the implications of the liberal study of the Bible for the formulation of Christian truth. Many theological students in preparing for ordination are taught a liberal view of the Bible, and are then introduced to a systematic theology which is all too often merely the elucidation of the thought of a particular epoch, buttressed by proof-texts from the Scriptures. Is not this kind of working out of doctrine a sort of game in which all compete and all win prizes, but in which the different players are competing according to differing rules, largely of their own invention? The study of theology has declined from being the Queen of the Sciences to a professional concern which does not always command a great respect from the modern educated layman: 'a theological argument' is often a term of disapproval.

There are many who say that a work about the Church should be partly historical in the sense of providing an explanation of how it is that the Church has come to be where she now is, and partly a description and analysis of the present-day Church in her environment. It is often held that discussion about the unity of the Church and the possible reunion of Christians should not be divorced from reality, conducted almost entirely in theological terms, but should be concerned with the practical questions of the possibility and machinery of reunion.

As far back as 1912 William Temple, in his essay on the Church in *Foundations,* referred to this kind of attitude when writing about the conflict between the ideal and the actual, although he was not advocating a merely pragmatic view of the question. 'To us this sounds remote and unreal. We do not feel that death and sin are conquered in our lives; the vast chaos which for us represents the Church, with its hateful cleavages, its slow-moving machinery, its pedantic antiquarianism, its indifference to much that is fundamental, its age-long ineffectiveness, its abundant capacity 'for taking the wrong side in moral issues—how can this be described in the language of St. Paul?' [1]

There can be no full examination of the doctrine of the Church which does not take into account the fact of the existence of the Church of South India, with its witness to the faith and courage which has enabled men and women to distinguish between essential theological principle and the prejudice caused by historical tradition. There will be other schemes and other reunions of Christians which will differ in detail from South India, but they will all be indebted to it. In view of the world-wide nature of the Christian Church and the emergence of the younger Churches to an adult position in the Church and in the world the attention of an unprejudiced observer must move away from the traditional centres of Christian thought and tradition, Rome and Geneva and Canterbury, to take notice of new trends and new inspiration. Again, the generosity of American Christians and the vitality of eastern Churches and the quality of their life, often under persecution, create a situation in which we can no longer look to the Reformation or to the Council of Trent as exclusive reservoirs of material for the formulation of Christian ideas and as the sole fountainheads of inspiration.

Indeed a return to a more biblical theology, a theology which is that of the Bible and not one formed by dependence on isolated texts, and a moving away from the Greek influence which so early permeated Christian systematic thought, might suggest a philosophy of activity rather than one of being. In that case one would become impatient with much earlier thought about the Church, and much more concerned to know what Christians are doing in the world in their own persons and in their own vocations—and need the example presented to us be always that of the Christian trades-unionist? Why not a Christian stock-broker or a Christian High Court Judge? Is not the work of the World Council of Churches in the sphere of help to refugees, Christian aid to the hungry, and help to underdeveloped countries a true expression of the charity, the agape, which is the essence of the Church as the Body of Christ in the world, expressed in terms of activity?

Dr. A. R. Vidler, at the beginning of his essay on 'Religion and the National Church,' [2] refers to the commonly held idea that the Church is a 'religious organization.' As he shows, it is all too often true. It is so fatally easy to organize and in so doing transform almost out of recognition the life and manifestation of the Spirit. It is only too easy for devotees to see their Christian duties in exclusively 'churchy' or pious activities. The Church is not an organization, however, founded by men, like some club, for specific purposes which were to be fulfilled by it, such as providing services which people might attend. Because Christians are Christians they will want to worship God; because they belong to the Church they will want to worship him corporately; but this is different from saying that the Church exists for the purpose of providing spiritual refreshment. Not only has the order of importance been inverted, but the obligation of the Church to witness and to serve has been forgotten.

The Church is the Christian Church. While we hope and pray and work for the eventual unity of all Christians, a unity which may express itself in common worship as well as common activity, we do not necessarily hope for a future common religion for the whole world, if by a common religion we mean a mixture of all the major faiths of the world, bringing in the good points of all. It would be impossible to amalgamate the various forms of belief and worship, and at the same time retain the distinctive characters of any of them—except possibly Buddhism. Buddhism has the greatest power of absorption and adaptation; but Buddhism digests as well as absorbs, and in the end there would be a reformed Buddhism which essentially had remained unchanged; but it would certainly not be Christianity, even though it contained, as Buddhism undoubtedly does contain now, some Christian elements. If the hope is for a future world-religion, then it must be one of the present faiths, or a completely new faith, invented, or evolving naturally out of the present religious beliefs and customs of men.

There may be a necessary dialogue with other faiths. Christians must not be arrogant or supercilious in their approach to those whose faith is different from theirs (how could they show such attitudes and still remain representatives of the Christian faith?).

But they may believe that God has spoken to men through Christ, and that the Christian revelation is of a higher order than other ways to God.

But what are we to say of the fellowship of those who call themselves Christians—if we may use the word fellowship of the diversity of men constituting different 'churches,' often hardly on speaking terms with one another? Is there, one wonders, a fellowship of the Holy Spirit which underlies or transcends our human barriers and divisions, so that men, although they think that they are separated, are really united in the Spirit, with the result that it is quite in order for us to go on using the words of 2 Cor. 13 : 14? It may be that the problem of Christian reunion is not to unite a broken Church, but to discover the essential unity of all Christian people to which we are blinded by our man-made distinctions between one Church and another.

It is not easy, however, to talk about the fellowship of all Christian people, or the problem of bringing together all Christian bodies, and be sure that we know exactly what we are discussing. The wording suggests that there is a division between those who are Christian and those who are not, that there is a division between those who are members of the Church and those who are not. Presumably there must be some division between Christian and non-Christian; the degrees of relevance to the main stream of historic Christianity shade off imperceptibly until one is faced with some odd variant of the Christian faith which one feels could never justifiably claim the name. But at the same time it would be most presumptuous to attempt to define where the line comes, to enable us to say that those on one side of the line are Christians in the Church, and that those on the other are non-Christians. This is the danger in interpreting belief in the 'one holy catholic and apostolic church' as though the words referred to an historic organized body visible and distinct in the world.

Not that one should reject belief in the Church as an institution in favour of an individualism which stresses merely the relationship between the individual man and Christ. The Reformation is often blamed for having caused a decay in beliefs about the Church, and for a decent godly order to have substituted an unlimited individualism based upon private and often wild interpretations of the Scriptures. This is not the case. It may be rather surprising to learn that one of the things which the Reformers had to do was to work out and present to their followers a doctrine of the Church, for this was something in which mediaeval Roman theology was deficient. There are reasons for this neglect, but the fact remains that St. Thomas Aquinas did not include in his *Summa* any systematic exposition of the doctrine of the Church. As a group of Evangelical theologians has put it: 'The prevalence of Greek rather than Hebrew modes of thought no doubt made the biblical concept of the People of God a difficult one; but perhaps the principal cause of the neglect was the actual dominance of the Church in individual and social life. A majestic society, claiming divine authority and unchallenged by serious rivals, made any doctrine of the Church in a sense superfluous.' [3] The companion Free Church Report on the doctrine of the Church, *The Catholicity of Protestantism*, makes a similar point, and gives details of what Luther and Calvin wrote about the Church. 'The whole Reformation movement may be fairly described as an attempt to take seriously the New Testament doctrine of the Church, actual, visible and catholic, as the fellowship of the Holy Spirit, in reaction from the medieval neglect of the Church.' [4]

In the Church of England the importance of the doctrine may be seen by the fact that Articles 19 to 34 deal with the Church, the sacramental life of the Church and her organization. The care with which the Ordinal of Edward VI was drawn up shows the concern of Thomas Cranmer and others for the historical continuity of the Church, a concern that the Church should survive as an organized, visible body, with Bishops, Priests and Deacons after the ancient pattern, ordained according to the ancient form, and with the ministry of Word and Sacrament perpetuated. The writings of the principal theologians of the period add their evidence to this. Witness these words of Bishop John Jewel, Bishop of Salisbury, writing in his *Apology* or Defence of the Church of England (English translation, 1564).

'Further, if we do shew it plain, that God's holy gospel, the ancient bishops, and the primitive church do make on our side, and that we have not without just cause left these men, and rather have returned to the apostles and old catholic fathers; and if we shall be found to do the same not colourably, or craftily, but in good faith before God, truly, honestly, clearly, and plainly; and if they themselves which fly our doctrine, and would be called catholics, shall manifestly see how all those titles of antiquity, whereof they boast so much, are quite shaken out of their hands . . .'

'We believe that there is one church of God, and that the same is not shut up (as in times past among the Jews) into some one corner or kingdom, but that it is catholic and universal, and dispersed throughout the whole world; so that there is now no nation which can truly complain that they be shut forth, and may not be one of the church and people of God; and that this church is the kingdom, the body, and the spouse of Christ; and that Christ alone is the prince of this kingdom; that Christ alone is the "head of this body; and that Christ alone is the bridegroom of this spouse."' [5]

The Church, in the intention of Jesus, is One. It is clear that it is the intention of Jesus that the Church should be one, that Christians should demonstrate the unity which is that of Christ with the Father. 'And the glory which thou hast given me I have given unto them; that they may be one, even as we are one . . . that they may be perfected into one' (John 17 : 22 and 23); cf. John 11 : 52—'that he might also gather together into one the children of God that are scattered abroad.'

This is the ideal, and much of the language of the New Testament about the Church is idealistic. It is the Body of Christ, it is his Bride, it is the New Israel. But the ideal is not realized, and we may compare with this situation the moral imperatives of Jesus, which are likewise the moral ideal. We do not obey him, do not keep his teaching on human behaviour, and yet we call ourselves Christians. The unity of the Church has been broken—it was threatened within the New Testament period, and soon began to be unrealizable. It was kept in being by rather desperate expedients, by declarations of heresy and of schism, long before the great schism between East and West in the eleventh century. But because schism and disunity have been there from the beginning the Church today is not absolved from the exercise of Christian charity, is not removed from the necessity of doing everything possible to bring together into a real unity members of differing Christian bodies.

I

We must be quite honest about the disunity of the visible Church. It is not sufficient to say, as the Revised Catechism of 1962 says on this point—

'By these words I mean that the Church is *One* because, in spite of its divisions, it is one family under one Father, whose purpose is to unite all men in Jesus Christ our Lord.' If these words be taken seriously they imply that there is a unity of the Church under one Father, so that the divisions may be ignored as not having shattered this unity. There is not a real unity at the present time; we assert our belief in the One Church in the Creed as a proclamation of our belief that this is Christ's intention, and that it is to this that we aspire.

We are reminded in *The Fulness of Christ*[6] that schism is not always wholly evil. 'When new insights are given and are rejected by the main body of the Church, it may be necessary that those to whom the new insights have been given should for the sake of the truth separate themselves from those who will not move forward with the Spirit of God.' Such a position, of course, must always be taken up in humility and after great heart-searching.

Next, the Church is Holy. The community of those who accept the Lordship of Jesus and who try to live out his teaching partakes of the holiness of God, in the same way that the moon reflects the light of the sun. There is no sanctity in the Church of herself; the quality of the lives of the members of the Church contributes nothing to the holiness of the members considered collectively. The members of the Church are saints, and 'saints' in the New Testament, as is well known, are not special members of the Church who are elevated to or recognized as possessing a superior quality of holiness; 'saints' are all those who make up the body of Christ, and the word refers to the status which they have been accorded rather than a quality which distinguishes their lives. But because the Church is the Church of God, gathered in obedience to his will, dedicated to carry out his work, then it is a holy fellowship.

This is one aspect of the word. In the Bible the word also refers to the quality of being set apart for the worship or service of God, and this quality of apartness, of being in the world but not of the world, is also a necessary quality of the Church. There is before the Church a problem of communication, of building bridges of understanding. The Church must make its contact with the world, and must serve the world. An incomprehensible Church, a Church turned in upon itself, serving only its own interests and answering its own parochial needs, is not a Christian Church. But although there must be a contact with the world and a communication, there must never be identification. This is one of the most difficult lessons which members of the Church must learn, and it must be learned through love, through a love of the neighbour which is never divorced from love of God.

The Church which is holy is a community. The Church is represented in Scripture as a fulfilment of God's purpose, a purpose which is revealed in community. There is a relation between God and the individual in the Bible, and the Bible contains a great deal of personal religion and personal apprehension of God. But these individuals are never isolated, and they always think of themselves as members of the people of God. God deals personally with his people, and he has personal relationships with each one of them, and yet they are all conscious that they are Israel, God's people. There is a priestly caste in the old Israel; the sons of Levi are concerned with the Temple. But they are designated for office, and their distinction is one of function. They are not spiritually superior, and have no spiritual advantage in relation to God. They are concerned with the Temple and with sacrificial worship; when the synagogue system developed the sons of Levi did not extend their function to take control of this non-Temple, non-sacrificial worship. Men might approach God through the synagogue worship, complementary to the Temple and not a substitute for it, without the benefit of the priestly caste.

Thus when Jesus began his Ministry he proclaimed his message, according to St. Mark, in the same terms of community—men are to repent because God's kingdom, God's kingly rule, is at hand (Mark 1:14, 15). The Son of Man has come to seek and save that which was lost (Luke 19:10). He will draw all men unto himself (John 12:32). He is the Shepherd who is to gather together the lost sheep of the house of Israel (Matt. 15:24; cf. John 10). When men respond to his message they are told to follow him; it is in their closeness to him that they realize their unity with each other. The teaching in the Acts of the Apostles about the Christian congregation, the Church, is a necessary development and fulfilment of the teaching of Jesus. It is not strange, as some theologians have thought, that the Kingdom, the *basileia,* is replaced by the Church, the *ecclesia.* It is in part a change of term, not a change of meaning, for the word *ecclesia,* with all its associations, was much more familiar to the Gentile world than the ideas connected with *basileia. Basileia* might have suggested political connections, and moreover the word has no Old Testament associations which would be valuable in a theological context, except connections with the Davidic hope. *Ecclesia,* however, with its connections with the Hebrew word for the congregation of Israel, for which it is the translation in the Greek version of the Old Testament, the Septuagint, is a much more suitable term in writing for Gentiles who knew their Old Testament. We must never forget that the Christian Church inherited a very great deal of missionary work which had been done among the Greek speaking Gentiles of the ancient world, for whose sake mainly the Old Testament had been translated into Greek in the second century B.C.

The term kingdom also reminds us that it is an eschatological term. Ever since the beginning of this century, as a result of the work of Johannes Weiss and Albert Schweitzer, it has been impossible to ignore the fact that Jewish apocalyptic theology and the Jewish apocalyptic books are a part and a very important part of the background of the New Testament, and that it is impossible to understand the Gospels without taking this into account. To ignore the eschatological element, or to transmute it into another idiom, is to distort the Gospel picture of Jesus and his message. The story of the Last Supper is the source of our authority for the continuance of the Sacrament of the Holy Communion in the life of the Church, but it is the occasion for the saying of Jesus that he would no more drink of the fruit of the vine until that day when he would drink it new in the kingdom of God (Mark 14:25).

But a comparison between the content of the Gospels and the writings of the Jewish apocalyptists serves to show quite conclusively that there are differences as well as similarities between the Jewish and the Christian works. In the Gospels is more than the Jewish hope that the sufferings of the present order would come to an end when God would set an end to history and inaugurate his kingdom, either on earth or in heaven. The Gospels, as Prof. F. C. Burkitt and Dr. C. H. Dodd have shown, assume that some things, to which the Jewish writers look forward, are already in the past, whilst others are still in the future.[7] The 'eschaton' in the Gospels is not just that which is the end of history, but that which intrudes into history. In the ministry of Jesus the power, the dunamis, of God is operative among men (Mark 1 : 27). By the finger of God he casts out demons and thus men know that the kingdom of God is among them (Luke 11 : 20). The power, the dunamis of God in the kingdom becomes in the Epistles the Spirit in the Church. The continuation of the Gospel, the proclamation of the Gospel by word and sacrament, means that the Church is not merely proclaiming a message but bearing witness to a power. The Holy Communion is a proclamation of the Lord's death until he come (1 Cor. 11 : 26). Nevertheless it is only in so far as the Church is faithful to the Gospel and partakes of the Holy Spirit that the Church is an eschatological body.

We are reminded also that when we speak of the Church, meaning the body of Christians dispersed throughout the world, we are making an assumption when we limit the significance of the word to those Christians who are now alive. Former Christians do not cease to be members of the Church because they have departed this earthly scene. Traditionally this has been recognized by the distinction between the Church militant and the Church triumphant, the Church on earth and the Church in heaven or Paradise. But clearly although we may recognize that we are compassed about with a cloud of witnesses, that our worship is with angels and archangels and with the whole company of heaven, we cannot even begin to make definitive statements about the Church triumphant. We cannot speak of its membership or the qualifications for being accepted in it; we can say nothing about its organization or its activity. We confess in the Creed that we believe in the communion of saints, the *communio sanctorum*, but we do not go on to define this faith further, and the brief reference stands alone. We believe that the *communio sanctorum* exists, but further than this there is little that we can say. The Revelation of St. John the Divine does not contain direct factual information bearing on the Church in heaven.

The Church is entrusted with the proclamation of the Gospel. Without discussing the old conundrum, which came first, the Church or the Gospel, we may say that there would be no reason for the existence of the Church in the world except as a guardian and transmitter of the Gospel, the *euangelion*, considered in its broadest aspects. For 'the Gospel' is not just the assertion that Christ died on the cross. When St. Paul said that we 'preach Christ crucified' he was not implying that the preaching was the bare assertion of the death of Christ for the sins of the world.

The Gospel is the whole of the saving work of Christ in personal and corporate terms, his life, death, resurrection and ascension; his teaching and example; the significance of all this as a fulfilment of the prophecies of the Old Testament, and a pointer to that which is in the future for each individual, the possibility of repentance and baptism into the new Community. The Gospel is proclaimed in word and sacrament; and as the Church and Gospel partake of the power of the age to come, so the sacraments are eschatological sacraments. Baptism is death and rebirth, incorporation into the Messiah (Rom. 6:1–11); the Holy Communion is a real fellowship with the Risen Christ, and looks forward to his return (1 Cor. 10:16–17).

It is now a commonplace to speak of the message of the Church as 'the proclamation,' the kerygma. From the Acts of the Apostles and the Epistles of St. Paul it was possible for Dr. C. H. Dodd to reconstruct the pattern of the primitive preaching.[8] It has a kind of credal ring, and it sets the Christian message within the context of the fulfilment of the Old Testament scriptures. Whilst it has a place for the story of the life and presumably the teaching of Jesus, it does not concentrate attention on the teaching and example of his life but speaks about Jesus as one who was performing a redemption.

Thirdly, the Church is Catholic and Apostolic. These words are pointers to the nature of the Church, but they are not descriptive of it without a great deal of further explanation, for both of these words have changed their meanings very considerably since the early days of Christianity. 'Catholic' has passed through at least three phases; from being the ordinary Greek adjective for 'universal' it came to have the meaning of 'orthodox' as compared with those churches or individuals departing from the main stream of the Christian faith, so that various notes of catholicity came to be defined. At a still later date it was maintained that 'catholicity' necessarily involved communion with and subservience to the Bishop of Rome. Thus Roman Catholic writers are quite right when they say that by definition those who are outside the Roman fellowship cannot be 'catholic,' and therefore cannot be of the Church. So also those Anglicans are right when they say by definition that Free Churchmen in England are deficient in their concept of catholicity since they do not possess the threefold ministry of Bishop, Priest and Deacon; the Free Churchmen are also right when they say that a local, national Church cannot be 'the Church catholic' because that term means a world-wide Church.

When we refer to the Church as apostolic we are using an adjective which in itself says nothing as to the meaning which attaches to it. Is the Church apostolic when it resembles the Church of the Apostles' day; or when it teaches the faith which was that of the Apostles; or when it has a ministry with historical succession from the time of the Apostles? All these are logically possible as the way in which the word might be used. Generally speaking it is used nowadays in two senses, by Catholics as referring to the apostolic succession in ordinations, or by Protestants as referring to the faithfulness of the Church in proclaiming the authentic apostolic Gospel.[9] There may be indeed a certain imponderable value in having an historical succession of ordinations from the time of the Apostles. But it needs to be demonstrated whether such a mechanical succession can of itself guarantee purity of doctrine or sincerity of life. It may, however, be possible to maintain that the Threefold Ministry has *in practice* an advantage over other forms of Church government (although we have in reality a twofold ministry in the Church of England, for the diaconate has no really independent life). The Threefold Ministry has been accepted in the Church of South India, and there is hope that the Threefold Ministry will form the basis of other schemes of union.[10] But already there are evidences that whilst many who were formerly in non-episcopal churches are willing to accept an episcopal form of government, it is much more difficult to get a united Church which is so formed to accept a particular theory of episcopacy. Unless it is held that episcopacy is of the *esse* of the Church, and that a particular theory of it is to be related to a doctrine of the Church, this must be so. The Anglican Communion is not committed to a particular theory of episcopacy; the majority view in our Church is that episcopacy is of the *bene esse* or the *plene esse* of the Church. But differing interpretations of the threefold ministry are held by individuals within our borders.[11]

It cannot be maintained on historical evidence, largely because of the fragmentary nature of the evidence for the ministry between the New Testament and the end of the second century, that the apostolic succession has been held in unbroken line from the days of the Apostles. Likewise because of the evidence it cannot be demonstrated that in the first one hundred and fifty years of Christian history men sat lightly to the need for a solemn ordering of the ministers of the Church by those who held the highest authority in the Church. The churches which claim the title 'catholic and apostolic,' and which use these terms in the forefront of their claims, are concerned that ordination shall be by Bishops; that the ancient credal formularies should be held, the Holy Scriptures venerated, and the sacraments of Christ should be observed. There may be differences in the number of the sacraments, in the theory of orders, in the practice of ordination, and in particular words in the Creeds, but generally speaking these are held to be the marks of catholic and apostolic order.

What we need to do is to come to an understanding not of what the words 'catholic' and 'apostolic' mean, but to agree as to the sense in which we are going to use them. It is useless to argue about their 'correct' meaning, for in the course of history they have been made to mean different things according to the climate of opinion. We need to begin again, retracing our steps as far back as we can in the history of the Church, not in order to ignore the whole of Christian history and rely only on the Scriptures, but in order that we may work out for ourselves anew meanings which we may all attach to the old words which have served for so long to divide us, and to get to understand what in the providence of God is a Church which is one, holy, catholic and apostolic.

NOTES

[1] op. cit., p. 340.
[2] In *Soundings*, 1962.
[3] *The Fulness of Christ*, 1950, p. 30.
[4] op. cit., p. 91.
[5] *Apology*, Parker Society edition, pp. 56, 59.
[6] p. 9.
[7] See the history of the interpretation of the concept by Norman Perrin in *The Kingdom of God in the Teaching of Jesus* (1963).
[8] In *The Apostolic Preaching* (1936). More recently, the tendency is to speak of the N.T. Kerygmata (plural), but this does not affect the argument above.
[9] See the discussion in J. R. Nelson, *The Realm of Redemption*, 1951, pp. 150–9.
[10] Cf. Bishop A. C. Headlam: 'It is not because I believe that the historical episcopacy is necessary for valid orders, but because I believe that it is necessary to secure Christian unity, that I hold that it must be the rule of a reunited Church.'
[11] cf. *The Apostolic Ministry*, ed. by K. E. Kirk, 3rd ed. 1957;
The Historic Episcopate, ed. by K. M. Carey, 1954;
The Apostolic Succession, by A. Ehrhardt, 1953;
Apostle and Bishop, by A. G. Hebert, 1963.

FROM ANGLICAN SYMBIOSIS TO
ANGLICAN SYNTHESIS

by

EMMANUEL AMAND DE MENDIETA

FROM ANGLICAN SYMBIOSIS TO
ANGLICAN SYNTHESIS

THIS essay is intended to popularize certain ideas and hopes which are, I believe, true and inspiring. It was first delivered, and afterwards written, with the fervent desire to contribute to a small extent to the speeding up of the current process of internal reconciliation, and to the growth of mutual trust and brotherly love between the various tendencies, wings or schools of thought in the Church of England of today.

There have now been admitted into this Church a number of people who were obliged for reasons of conscience, though not without sadness, to leave the Roman Catholic Church. For many of them—priests and laymen—it was a painful shock to find out that so many clergymen and laymen of this divided Church of England are still living, in their mutual relationships, on rather unfriendly terms, *comme chien et chat*. I know for instance that in one large city, the Vicar of a very low Parish Church, an extreme Evangelical himself, never exchanges a greeting, even a simple 'Hullo,' or a polite word, with another colleague, an honorary Canon and Vicar of a high Parish Church. They go on completely ignoring one another, year after year!

The plain and unpalatable truth is that, even in the sixties and in our ecumenical era, the Church of England remains painfully divided in many areas and circles. Many clergymen, and in higher proportion many laymen, belonging to divers tendencies or parties, do not have enough mutual trust, esteem and love, to enter in a real intercourse of full collaboration, and true brotherly and Christian charity. Too many of my Anglican fellow-Christians go on living, as their parents and ancestors did, as quarrelsome, quibbling and pugnacious brothers and sisters. Anglo-Catholics and Evangelicals share indeed the same Anglican heritage, but too many of them share it in a quite arbitrary and disastrous manner. Sectarian Anglo-Catholics claim to possess all the Catholic heritage, whereas narrow-minded Evangelicals are satisfied with the particular doctrines, rites (and prejudices) of the Reformers of the sixteenth century.

What a pity it is to discover that some Anglo-Catholic priests give the first priority to the wearing of ugly things, like birettas and cottas, and to extra-liturgical devotions in the honour of the Blessed Sacrament! But equally what a pity to observe the dislike, sometimes the horror, of many Evangelical incumbents for the wearing of beautiful and traditional Eucharistic vestments! Many of them still maintain a fierce and dogged resistance to the urgent and necessary revision of the utterly antiquated and unsatisfactory Eucharistic rite of the 1662 Prayer Book.

In this essay, I shall try to sketch a rough picture of the historic destiny of Anglicanism. I shall start with a short assessment of the Anglican Reformation in the sixteenth century. Then I shall venture to describe the sociological phenomenon of the past and present Anglican *symbiosis* or co-existence. Finally I shall suggest the twofold aim of the Anglican *synthesis:* on the one hand, to attain a wider theological agreement and a stronger Church unity through dialectical debates, and, on the other hand, to reach a powerful increase of mutual and sincere Christian love.

I

THE ANGLICAN REFORMATION

I am fully convinced that, considered from the point of view of its *positive* content, the Reformation of the sixteenth century contains no essentially anti-Catholic element. In so far as it was a protest against anything, it was a protest, not against Catholicism, but against the Romanist attempt of subversion of something which is essential to the health and integrity of the Catholic faith, that is the sovereignty of God's grace and of the Gospel over the Christian 'religion,' and over the institutional structure of Christianity. Thus the historic Anglican decision to contain the Reformation protest, and to retain it within the context of Catholic faith and institutions, is not so strange and paradoxical a programme as it appears to so many Protestant and Roman Catholic observers. The Anglican Reformers, especially Archbishop Cranmer, wanted a new spirit but not a new theological system. They took advantage, of course, of a favourable historical and political situation, which made this experiment possible. The fact that this experiment was possible, and was indeed undertaken, may yet turn out to be the most fateful and important of all the developments which took place in the sixteenth century, in which violent nationalism combined with a vivid, but too often fanatical, Christian faith.

The very existence and success of the modern Anglican communion calls in question a maxim, which is too easily taken for granted both among Roman Catholics and among the great majority of Protestants. This maxim is as follows: the Catholic faith and the Reformation protest are logically incompatible, and therefore the line between them is an ultimate dividing line, which compels us to stand *either* on the one side, *or* the other. On the contrary, the very existence of our world-wide Anglican communion implies that the tragic division between the two sides (the Catholic faith and the Reformation protest) has resulted, not from any essential clash between irreducible principles in matters of faith, but rather from conflicting theological views or systems, and also from the sorrowful national and international accidents of sixteenth-century history. The emerging schisms were perpetuated by a mutual lack of love, sympathy and understanding, by a mutual fear, and by prejudices rather than by true insight and deep divergences in matters of faith. Above all, Anglicanism has no need of the negative theological ideologies, which, in the Reformation Churches, have constricted and confined, sometimes almost suffocated, the Reformation protest itself. For the real purpose of these negative ideologies has been to defend, not the prophetic Reformation protest itself properly understood, but the characteristic Reformation institutions. Lacking these characteristic institutions, the Anglican communion has no need of the negative theological ideologies which bolster them up. The positive values of the Reformation protest, the Anglican should claim, are stronger and healthier, precisely owing to the absence of these specific Reformation institutions. The burden of defending them is too heavy; the necessity of loyally maintaining them is too contrary to a true reconciliation of Christendom as a whole. The Reformation prophetic message sounds more purely and penetratingly, when it is purged of any sectional design to perpetuate the too revolutionary Reformation institutions.

Of course, to evaluate the Anglican Reformation in this way is not necessarily to adopt an uncritical attitude towards its positive performances. The precise details of the Anglican Reformation are not sacrosanct, even for Anglicans. I venture to submit the following statement. Under the influence of the violent emotions, hatreds and strong prejudices of that troubled time, the Anglican Reformation, while rightly professing an ideal of moderation, went indeed much further in a revolutionary direction than was either necessary or required by its own principles. Its purging or pruning of the mediaeval traditions not only eliminated what was certainly corrupt and harmful, but also many things that were, in their own way, valuable and worthy of preservation. Happily nothing essential to the integrity of the Catholic faith was sacrificed, but many desirable things were lost, so that a patient work of recovery had to be undertaken at a later date. And this was in fact done wholly within Anglicanism and with utter loyalty to the basic Anglican principles. This work of recovery has been the historic vocation of the so-called Anglo-Catholic movement. It seems to me obvious, for instance, that the Anglo-Catholic recovery of the solemn and moving Holy Week services of the Latin ancient and mediaeval Church, is pure spiritual gain, which needs neither apology nor defence. The Palm Sunday ceremonies (the blessing, distribution and procession of the palms), the magnificent rites of Maundy Thursday (the solemn Eucharist, the stripping of the altars, and the *Mandatum*), the beautiful Liturgy of Good Friday (especially the solemn prayers for the holy Church of God and all his ministers and members, the dramatic and moving veneration of the cross during the singing of the Reproaches, and the Liturgy of the Presanctified), and finally the solemn vigil of Easter Sunday, now happily restored during the night (with the blessings of the new fire, of the incense and of the paschal candle, during which the Deacon sings the triumphant *Exsultet* or the great lyrical Paschal proclamation)—all these beautiful and truly evangelical services were unfortunately surrendered or given up, owing to a negative Reformation prejudice. The Anglo-Catholic recovery of these beautiful services of the ancient Church in no way endangers any essential Reformation principle. On the contrary, once Anglicanism has completely recovered its right to use such splendid ceremonies as recognized forms of worship, ways of witness, and channels of teaching, this recovery, which is not at all a surrender of the essential principles of the Anglican Reformation, is a return to the best liturgical traditions of the Catholic Church, in closer conformity with these Reformation principles.

The same assessment might be made concerning the recovery of the Eucharistic vestments, which were traditional in all the Christian Churches of the East and of the West before the turmoil of the Reformation in the sixteenth century. These Eucharistic vestments emphasize the difference between the Lord's Supper, or the Eucharistic Liturgy, and other seemly forms of worship, as Matins and Evensong, designed, and indeed well designed, by men (in roughly their present form, by Cranmer) for the glory and praise of Almighty God. For this very reason, these services take place on a lower plane than the Divine and Eucharistic Liturgy, this great act of worship prescribed, for its essential act, by Jesus Christ himself, in the last Supper, for the salvation of men. *Do this in remembrance of me.*

The maintenance of the essential Anglican position would indeed be quite possible without the Anglo-Catholics, who have often been regarded as difficult and intransigent people, chiefly because they have often been in fact difficult and intransigent. Nevertheless the signs are that, without the Anglo-Catholic witness, Anglicanism tends to degenerate into a rather complacent and torpid mediocrity; without it, Anglicanism tends too easily to assume that we have already obtained the Anglican vision and fulness.

Similarly I would defend the position of the out-and-out Evangelical Anglicans in precisely the same way. In my view, and this is my thesis, the fulness of Anglicanism will be found at last not so much through the triumph of the 'centre' or of 'moderate' churchmanship, as through the meeting, merging, and *synthesis* of the extremes. The fulness of Anglicanism will be utterly catholic and uncompromisingly evangelical at the same time, all of the same breath. In other words, I should like to defend this idea: Anglicanism must grow out of a practical compromise and *symbiosis* into a vital and integrated *synthesis,* if its destiny is to be fulfilled.

This distinction between the Anglican compromise and the Anglican final synthesis is clearly discussed and illustrated by Professor J. V. L. Casserley in his excellent book, *Christian Community* (Longmans, 1960). Merely to seek a practical compromise between the two extremes is not only to steer a difficult course

K

between their errors and excesses; it is also to miss and ignore the great values of the two extremes. And indeed a mere compromise has characteristic defects and corruptions of its own. In spiritual matters, the real trouble about the *via media,* as a practical compromise, is its chronic tendency towards complacency and mediocrity. 'In trying to steer a middle way between catholic and evangelical Christianity, it may well miss the depths and treasures of both, and end up in an unlovely mood of smug superiority, which the middle position, considered in itself, does nothing to justify. Anglicans must not acquiesce in a situation, in which they are *rather* Evangelical and *rather* Catholic, more Evangelical than the Catholics, but not so Evangelical as the Evangelicals, and more Catholic than the Evangelicals, but not so Catholic as the Catholics. Our aim in Anglicanism must be to become extreme Evangelicals, and extreme Catholics at the same time.' [1] Only so can we hope to inherit, exemplify and proclaim in our lives both the fulness and sovereignty of the Gospel, and also the wholeness of the Catholic faith in our Christian life and action.

II

THE ANGLICAN SYMBIOSIS OR NECESSARY CO-EXISTENCE

Now at the beginning of the second part of this essay,[2] a part dealing with the actual Anglican *symbiosis,* or vital and harmonious co-existence, I ask a sociological question, not a theological one. I am not asking: 'By what theological common doctrine are the members of the Church of England held together?', but: 'In the eventual absence of a very large extent of common theological doctrine, by what bond are the members of the Church of England held together?'

It is not enough to seek the answer merely in the Establishment, or more generally in the close bonds which have linked the Church of England with the history and life of the English people. The evidence that this answer is insufficient lies in the world-wide Anglican Communion. No part or province of it is 'established' except the two provinces of Canterbury and York. In many regions of the world, it is a minority among Christians, and even a tiny minority. It includes many members who are not, even remotely, of English origin, whose history and culture are in no way connected with the past history of the Church in England. In this world-wide communion of Christian people, the same diversities which we find in England are reproduced on a wider scale, and the same bewildering phenomenon of unity in diversity. This is obviously not due to the political and social conditions prevailing in England. It must be due to something which is characteristic of the Anglican way of life.

The Anglican unity, in its present *symbiosis*, is a unity of spirit. That is the point from which we must start. Anglicans *feel* that they belong together, and that their association or fellowship is a good thing, which they are determined to preserve. But it is essentially a unity in diversity, in difference, and it would lose its point if the differences were to disappear. This is not to say that some differences or diversities ought not to disappear. Thus, it would no doubt be better if there were more agreement, more of a common mind, especially in matters of theology, in the Church of England. But, in that case, the Church of England would no longer be what it happens to be, and it is the Church of England, as it now is, that we are trying to understand as a sociological phenomenon.

Our next question then must be: On what footing is this vital co-existence, this *symbiosis* of diversities, made possible? And here we must duly observe the peculiar form which the diversity of outlook and opinion takes in the Church of England. 'The spectrum of Anglican belief and behaviour presents a continuous and unbroken series of hues or nuances, from one extreme to the other. Talk of the two "wings" or "parties" in our Church can often mislead the non-Anglican on this point. The great majority of Anglicans do not think of themselves as definite party men. They cluster in large numbers round a central position, which defies logical definition, but whose flavour is clearly recognizable, and they thin out very considerably as one approaches the two extremes.' [3] The individual Anglican may move in such and such direction, in the course of his lifetime; he may cross over from one side of the centre to the other; he may go enthusiastically to one of the extremes; and yet he remains all the time within the Anglican fold.

Now I ask another question, which is as follows: 'What is it that is common to Anglicans, to all the members of the Anglican Communion, and also distinctive of them?' The answer here lies,

I think, in the field of public worship rather than of explicit and clearly defined dogma and accepted theology. It lies in the use of a common liturgy. In the last resort, an Anglican is one who will use the liturgy (in the broad sense of the term) provided in the Prayer Book of 1662 or 1928 (including the Ordinal), if he is English; or one of that family of liturgies which have sprung from the first or the second Cranmer's Prayer Books, if he is not English. He may modify the official or 'legal' Prayer Book of his own Church in using it, as many of us do in England; he may quarrel with other Anglicans about the right interpretation of it. But, if he uses the Prayer Book of his own Anglican Church,[4] he is an Anglican, and, if he will not use it, there is no legitimate place for him in the Anglican fellowship.

Anglicans of England are deeply conscious of unity not only with one another in the present, but also with the past history of the Church in their own land. They feel themselves at one with the English Christians of Anglo-Saxon and mediaeval times, not only by virtue of holding a common faith, but also by virtue of membership in the same Church. The Church of England is vividly conscious of its unbroken continuity with the Church of St. Augustine of Canterbury, of St. Theodore, of St. Dunstan, of Edward the Confessor, of the archbishops, Anselm, Thomas Becket and Langton.

Unquestionably the Church of England underwent a revolutionary and rather violent change in the sixteenth century, and all its subsequent history has been conditioned by what took place then. But a revolution does not inevitably destroy the identity of the institution which undergoes it. The Church of England has changed no more, and probably less, than the political institutions of England, and it has never lost its sense of the past. This point needs no explanation for those who know the atmosphere of the Free Churches, where there is no vivid awareness of anything in Christian history or tradition that is earlier than the sixteenth century.

It cannot be denied that, in the Church of England, there is some Catholic continuity. What has surely survived the storm and earthquake of the Reformation, is a worshipping community of Christians, embracing, until about a century ago, the great bulk of the English people, governed by Bishops occupying the historic sees of England, and carefully preserving an episcopal succession by the laying on of hands, which links the contemporary Bishops with the mediaeval English hierarchy. The Anglican liturgy is derived from Catholic and Latin Missals and other service-books, by way of translation, paraphrase, abbreviation, and . . . omission. The Anglicans use the same sacraments and the same rites which were used in mediaeval England. They believe themselves to be carrying on the true tradition of the faith of the Catholic Church, only purged of certain Roman or Papal innovations, which they believe to be doctrinal deviations. The Anglicans show a persistent tendency to defend their peculiar position by appealing to the Fathers. This appeal brings them on to common ground with the Orthodox Church and with the Roman Catholic Church.

'The continuation of the hierarchy, on which so much depends, was made possible by the co-operation of the Crown with the Church's leaders. To the same influence is due the fact that the Church of England emerged from the Reformation uncommitted to any precise and clear-cut new theological system. The English Reformation does not bear the impress of any one masterful mind as Luther, Calvin or Zwingli. No single theologian of genius has so dominated our Church, as to give his name to it and impose his system upon it.' [5] Archbishop Cranmer came nearest to doing so, since he gave us our liturgy and shaped our forms of worship. The influence of the second Cranmerian Prayer Book (1552) on the Church of England far exceeds that of other Reformation documents (the Thirty-nine Articles being included), and every English Anglican has felt it. Yet, while we use Cranmer's liturgy, we interpret and adapt it as we wish. Who, apart from theological specialists, knows all the divers stages of the evolution of Cranmer's own eucharistic doctrine? In any case, he was an outstanding liturgiologist, but not a great systematic theologian. Hooker, too, the most influential theoretical writer of the Reformation period, is not so much the creator of a theological system as the interpreter and defender of what was by his time an established fact, namely the way of life into which the Church of England had settled down. And, influential though he is, the Church has never committed itself to his views. We are not the Cranmerian or the Hookerian Church, but the Church of England.

A clear evidence of the wisdom of those who guided the Church of England through the turmoil of the Reformation, was that 'they did not adopt a cut and dried theological system from abroad, nor did they produce one of their own. They made decisions where decisions were necessary, but they were not hasty to define what could be left undefined. And therefore they made the Church of England flexible and adaptable, like the English political system, open at once to the past and to the future, capable of bold initiatives and experiments, capable also of startling revivals of forgotten beliefs and practices, a living body and not a mechanical system.' [6]

Some people like to describe the Church of England as 'the Anglo-Saxon compromise.' It is a phrase which comes spontaneously to the mind in the present context. After all, it is notorious that the English are given to compromise in their practical affairs; a great part of their political genius is believed to consist in this. Have not the Anglicans themselves sometimes described their way of faith and life as a *via media?* And what is a *via media* but a happy compromise between two extremes?

Yes, but we must consider more closely the meaning of this kind of compromise in the Church of England, as it now is. What in fact is a compromise? In the proper sense of the word, it is an arrangement, whereby two or more conflicting parties reach a practical *modus vivendi* by mutual concessions. What kind of concessions are we to suppose lie at the basis of the Anglican 'compromise'? Not concessions of theological principle. The parties in the Church do not refrain from embracing what appears to them to be the theological truth, out of regard for one another's opinions; nor do they conceal their beliefs. It would be indeed scandalous if they did either of these things. The sphere, in which the concessions are made, is not that of theological essentials or fundamentals, but that of the outward forms in which they are stated. In other words, this sphere of compromise is only that of the wording of official documents, the selection of language, the use or non-use of devotional observances, which are not essential and would be offensive, and so on. We have all been taught that the English Prayer Book (1662) and the Thirty-nine Articles of Religion were deliberately so phrased that Catholics and Protestants alike could interpret them in their own way, and this deliberate ambiguity alone makes the Anglican peaceful *symbiosis* possible. Similarly the occasional efforts of episcopal authority to regulate or forbid certain devotional usages have this kind of meaning. Some particular practice, which may perhaps be justifiable and even profitable in itself, must yet be avoided, if it imperils the precarious unity of the whole body of the Church.

This does indeed explain how this Church of England holds together; and it also explains why the Anglican unity, wide as its range may be, has yet definite limits. There are large bodies of Christian people who can neither find nor desire any place in such a Church as the Church of England. Such is, of course, the case of the convinced Roman Catholic, especially if he is English or Irish. Such is also the case of that rigid-minded type of Romanist Anglo-Catholic, who is situated in the extreme right wing of the Church of England, and who is attracted to Rome, precisely by the appearance she presents of monolithic cohesion, definiteness and inflexibility. Such again is the Calvinist who thinks that Calvin is not improved by Anglican editing and toning down; he is likely to become a Presbyterian. And there are those who have found the full logical consequences of Protestant principle embodied in the Puritan conception of a 'gathered Church.' Here is a body of ideas which is as characteristic of Anglo-Saxon Protestantism, as the Lutheran and Calvinist systems are of the continental variety. It defines the Church not in terms of hierarchy or sacraments, nor even of the preaching of the Word, but in terms of the personal response of faith to the Word. The 'gathered Churches' present in their own life the picture of a local theocratic democracy, and it is difficult to see how even the Anglican genius for ambiguity could find formulae and institutions which would enable the Congregationalist and the Catholic to live permanently and happily together. The founding fathers of the Free Churches considered it to be impossible, and drew the conclusion by seceding from the Church of England.

In this second part of this essay, I have tried to understand the actual Church of England as a social phenomenon, and I have ventured to present a sketch of the peaceful *symbiosis* or vital co-existence of the Anglicans in the contemporary Church of England. This second part was rather a historical and social description of the behaviour of contemporary Anglicans, especially of those who are members of the Church of England. *Symbiosis,* or vital co-existence, though not without mutual tensions, were the key-words of this discussion.

III

THEOLOGICAL SYNTHESIS

Now let us proceed to the third part of this essay, in which we shall deal with a theological question, the Anglican *synthesis*. Is a genuine theological *synthesis* really possible in the Church of England of today and of tomorrow, and, in a more general manner, in the Anglican Communion at large? I shall thus attempt to analyse and define this ideal of *Anglican synthesis* between what is true and vital in Catholicism, and what is true and vital in Protestantism.

But, before I attempt to consider this theological problem of Anglican *synthesis,* I ought to answer an important question, and this answer will be the obvious introduction to the discussion of our theological problem.

Here is the question. 'Is there, in the present Church of England, a genuine and charitable zeal for dogmatic and theological truth? How do the theologians of this divided Church regard their own theological divisions? Do they take them for granted, as something quite in the order of things, which presents no particular challenge to them as Anglicans? Or, if they see the situation as a challenging one, how do they meet the challenge? Does each party embark upon a campaign to drive the others out of the Church, and to brand them as heretics, or to convert them entirely to its own point of view? Or, on the contrary, do the Anglican theologians cultivate that most difficult, though most precious, art of listening to one another with open minds (so far as human frailty can compass it), in common dependence upon the Holy Spirit?'[7]

It seems to me that the answer to these questions is not altogether a disgraceful or a negative one. The atmosphere within the Church of England, and also within the Anglican Communion as a whole, is nowadays not altogether unhealthy. Assuredly, in the Church of England, there are lively theological controversies and free exchanges of views. Of these there are many recent examples: the brisk discussions on the Open Letter of the thirty-two Theologians on Intercommunion, the appearance on television[8] of Dr. Vidler and his conversation with Mr. Ferris and Mr. Kennedy, and finally the outburst of enthusiasm and also of indignation raised up by the publication of *Honest to God,* the paper-back written by Dr. John A. T. Robinson, Bishop of Wool-wich. But, in spite of occasional impassioned and irresponsible mutual condemnations, we may assert that there exists in the Church of England of the second half of the twentieth century a real desire for better mutual understanding. It is not irrelevant to point out here that Anglicans over all the world have played and continue to play in the Ecumenical Movement a part which is out of all proportion to their numbers. And this is quite understandable since the Anglican Communion is a kind of Ecumenical Movement in itself.

All this does seem to show that there is an appreciation of the unique condition on which the Anglican way, and the institutional unity which it secures, can be theologically defensible. This institutional unity lived in *symbiosis* can be defended theologically *only if* this precarious unity of worship, collaboration and common will to live together within the same Church is used as a providential opportunity for the parties to grow together in understanding, in mutual esteem and love, and in progressive agreement in theological matters. Diversity can indeed be a good thing; it can be an enrichment to the Church to have within it divers traditions of theological thought, and of liturgical and devotional practice. But this diversity is only an enrichment if these traditions are felt as complementary to one another, and can be unified by the Church into one coherent body of thought or doctrine, and life.

I proceed therefore to a dialectical examination of our theological problem, namely the problem of Anglican *synthesis*. I am convinced that the historic mission or destiny of the Church of England, and, on a wider scale, the destiny of the world-wide Anglican Communion, is to make a theological and also a practical *synthesis* of Catholicism and Protestantism. This is the inner meaning of the stale and trite phrase 'Catholic and Reformed.' The idea of such a *synthesis* is not a new one. A writer has described the theology of John Wesley as 'an original and unique synthesis of the Protestant ethic of grace with the Catholic ethic of holiness.' This synthesis, if such it really was, took shape in the Church of England. I presume that Anglicanism and Methodism might both have been the richer, if Methodism had stayed in the mother Church.

'Again, in the lengthening perspective of time, the eminence of F. D. Maurice and the seminal character of his work become increasingly evident, and it has even been suggested that we should see in him a typical instance of what an Anglican theologian should be. But, of course, the ruling characteristic of Maurice's thinking is his perpetual effort to bring opposite views to a synthesis, including not only the various types of Protestantism, but also the true Catholic tradition, as he understood it.' [9] He was essentially a man at once utterly Evangelical and utterly Catholic, utterly Catholic because he was utterly Evangelical, and utterly Evangelical because he was utterly Catholic. Nearer to our own time, we may select the figure of Archbishop William Temple, a kind of God-intoxicated humanist, responsive to the guidance of God in almost every area of his complex, widely concerned life. In his life and writings, we can find a clue to the nature and future of the Anglican theology, way of life, and Communion. In such men as Maurice and Temple, Anglicanism ceases to be a mediocre, lukewarm and complacent middle way. Rather it becomes a total way, not steering between the extremes, but rather drawing together and uniting the positive values of what we may call the opposite poles of our Western Christendom.

Wesley, Maurice and Temple, in other things so unlike, are alike in this, that any of them could not have done what he did elsewhere except in the Church of England. Are we to say then that the very meaning of Anglicanism lies in the hope of making this theological and practical synthesis? Yes.

But, if we examine the problem of a possible *synthesis* between the Catholic and Protestant traditions, or, more accurately, between their theological systems, we ought to have clear notions about the characteristic features of these two theological systems.

These systematic structures are very different indeed from 'Catholicism' and 'Protestantism' considered as living realities. As living realities, both of them are based on a common principle or rather on a common divine work, namely the grace of the Lord Jesus Christ present and active in the power of the Holy Spirit. It is this reconciling grace which is at work on both sides, which creates the *one* Christian character of life and action, on both sides; which makes it possible for both sides to use common prayers, hymns, theological and devotional books. In our ecumenical era, we need, in all our separated Churches, a positive and constructive theology, which can do justice to all that is already tending to unite Catholics and Protestants.

But let us return to a brief consideration of the characteristic features of the two theological systems, as systems.

Catholicism (and not only Roman Catholicism) as a logical whole, and Protestantism as a logical whole, are two theological systems built on different principles. And even those doctrines and observances, which belong to both, may appear in a different perspective, and have a different meaning in the two systems. What are the underlying principles of these two theological systems?

The Catholic principle is that of fulness or comprehensiveness. If there is a sense in which 'comprehensiveness' is an Anglican ideal, there is a much deeper and truer sense in which it is the heart of Catholicism. 'The true Catholic Faith is that faith which embraces the whole revelation of God for all sorts and conditions of men, and the true Catholic Church is that Church which is the right one for all men, everywhere and always. Catholicity means holding to the fulness of the Faith, and heresy is the substitution of partial views for the whole. This is the principle to which Rome in her wiser moments appeals. And those in the Church of England or in the Orthodox Church, who contend that Roman Catholicism is not the true and full Catholicism, do so by turning Rome's own principle against her, arguing that she professes to have the whole Faith, but in fact falls short of this fulness.' [10]

A different principle lies at the heart of Protestantism. It is not by pure chance that Protestantism was historically manifested as a 'Reformation,' for the idea of purity, with the accompanying fear of corruption, dominates Protestant systematic theology, as the idea of fulness, with the accompanying fear of sectionalism or schism, dominates the Catholic outlook. The idea of purity is in itself a useful, nay a necessary and a noble idea. It plays a great part in the Catholic scheme of things also, especially in the discipline of the spiritual life and of monasticism. But it is not the ruling principle of the whole Catholic system. Protestantism makes it the ruling criterion, with revolutionary results.

In other terms, the theological principle of Protestantism, at its best, is perhaps a vivid and demanding sense of priorities. As such, this principle should be a corrective one (very necessary indeed), but not a constitutive one. It seems to me that the real heart of what is *positive* in Protestantism is not its protest against such and such Roman Catholic (or Orthodox) error and deviation, but its impassioned insistence on the freedom and sovereignty of God's grace, and on the centrality of Christ, its emphasis on the fact that everything has to be seen and appreciated in relation to God's reconciling grace in Christ.

Behind this conflict of theological principles, it is possible to detect something deeper and still more intractable, a conflict of mentality and outlook, of almost unconsciously underlying attitudes and reactions against doctrines and traditions of the 'others.' In his booklet already quoted, *Anglicanism and Orthodoxy,* Professor H. A. Hodges made a penetrating analysis of this conflict of mentality and outlook, which differentiates Protestants from Catholics.[11]

It is only if we take into consideration this conflict of mentality and outlook that we could understand the partly ambiguous and partly erroneous character of Protestantism. Many of the central affirmations of the Christian faith are present in it, and firmly kept and proclaimed. But, side by side with them, we also find that spirit of suspicion and denial, which determines the Protestant attitude to so many things in Catholic thought and life. Even the affirmations themselves are frequently made into denials; they are flung out as protests and manifestoes against something. The Protestant protestation of faith is also a protest against other people's faith. Some of us detect in some Lutheran and Reformed (or Calvinist) writers a certain nagging or hectoring tone. Their own faith is so negatively centred on the denial of one fundamental 'error,' that they see this 'error' in everything which other Christians say or do. Unhappily this spirit of negativism is very near the heart of the Protestant theological *system*. Therefore we cannot be surprised to find out that Protestant mentality gave birth to rationalism and liberalism, and finally to secular humanism. The present day attempt to stop the world-wide Protestant decline by returning to the Reformers, will prove abortive, unless the clock is put back further still, behind the Reformation and behind the later Western mediaeval Catholicism, which provoked the Reformers' rebellion.

Of course, to say that the Protestant system is infected with error is not to say that pre-Reformation Western Catholicism was free from error. It was not; and post-Reformation Roman Catholicism is still not free from error. Rich in her treasures of Christian faith and life, adorned with the holiness of many of her children, and strong in her continuity with the past, Rome, even Rome, has nevertheless a spirit of error within her, and this too, in its own way, is a spirit of negation. It is seen in the authoritarian tone adopted by the Papacy until John XXIII and also by the Roman Catholic hierarchy, the impatience of any free criticism, and the distrust of any show of legitimate independence. The teaching of the Encyclical *Humani Generis* (1950) is a painful reminder of this tendency.[12]

'Both the Catholic and the Protestant theological systems contain certainly something true and good, but both in their expressions are capable of serious degeneration. The first problem therefore is a critical one: it is to discriminate, to sift, to determine where each theological system has in fact degenerated, and to restore it to its true and proper form. This in itself is not an easy task, no short-term enterprise. But this is not the whole of what needs to be done. For, when the Catholic principle and the Protestant principle are each seen in their best light, the real problem will at last confront us: what is the right relation between these two theological principles, and between the two attitudes which underlie them, in a healthy system of Christian thought and life? Which is primary and which is subordinate? For, that was precisely the fundamental question of the Reformation, and it is a question to which the answer cannot be given in the form of a synthesis.'[13]

The thesis which I should like to submit is formulated in two propositions. The first one is that the Catholic principle of fulness or comprehensiveness, and the Protestant principle of purity, or rather of a vivid sense of priorities, can and must find their place together in a healthy and balanced Christian *synthesis*. My second proposition is that actual Catholicism and actual Protestantism, *as contending global theological systems,* represent in very fact incompatible ways of determining the balance.

At this stage, it is essential to emphasize the liberating distinction between faith and theology, especially between faith and theological system. The real and deep Church unity is one of faith, of life, and of sacramental worship; not of theological system. It is more and more recognized by theologians of many Churches that the classical Lutheranism and Calvinism, as theological systems, were very close to the mediaeval and Counter-Reformation scholastic systems. In both cases, there has been a failure to distinguish properly between the level of faith, and the level of theological reflection and systematization. In Christendom, theology is necessary but secondary, but divine faith is necessary and primary and essential.

Meanwhile, in the Eastern Orthodox Church, the apostolic faith has lived on, substantially unaffected by either Papal or Protestant innovations or deviations. This Church presents to us the faith and life of the ancient and undivided Church, not as a historical memory, but as a present fact. Speaking on the level of faith, not of theological systematization, and not on an empirical or practical level, I dare assert, with Professor H. A. Hodges,[14] that the Orthodox faith, that faith to which the Orthodox Fathers bear witness, and of which the Orthodox Church is the abiding keeper, is the Christian faith in its true and essential form, to which we all aspire and by which we are all judged. Another fact, which is surely less important, is that the Eastern Orthodox Church shows us the meaning of a non-Papal Catholicism, not as a theoretical possibility but as an actual fact.

By this we, Western Christians, can take our bearings. With this in mind, we can analyse our Western conflicting theological systems, in all of which truth is mingled with error (though not everywhere in the same proportions). With this conception of the Orthodox faith in mind, as a norm, we may set aside what is false in each Western theological system; we may keep what is true, and think it again in its proper context, which will be that of a lively and rediscovered Orthodoxy for the spiritual benefit of all Western Christians.

If this is the true account of what needs to be done, it is still true that Anglican theologians, and not only the theologians of the Church of England, are in a better position to do it than any other Christians in the West. Only it is a more painful task than is suggested by the easy and conventional phrases we sometimes hear about 'Anglican synthesis between Catholicism and Protestantism.' The real and difficult Anglican *synthesis* is one which must be fought for, in matters of faith and theology. The true *synthesis* is not a synthesis of Roman Catholicism and Protestantism as such, or more precisely of Roman Catholic and Protestant theological systems: they are incompatible. The true Anglican theological *synthesis* is only the synthesis of what is true in the *living* Roman Catholicism, and of what is true in the *living* Protestantism, and in other elements of truth which both have almost forgotten and are still kept in the Orthodox Church.

It is in a dialectical debate that it will be possible to determine the conditions and the ingredients of this Anglican *synthesis*. This dialectical debate is not a dispute in which the actual parties in the Church of England are ranged squarely against one another, but rather in which each party is ranged partly against itself, in a joint and serene search for a theological truth which transcends them. This kind of *multilateral* debate is called in philosophical language 'dialectic,' and this dialectical way is the way of mutual openness combined with fundamental analysis and self-criticism.[15] If this dialectic debate is what we are to expect in the Church of England today, we can characterize this Church of England as the pre-eminently dialectical Church of Christendom. If this Church is, in this way, the theatre or the field of a continuing dialectic and multilateral debate, things may happen in it which will be of significance far beyond its borders.

I must confess that this conception of the Church of England as the dialectical centre of the Western Christendom may seem a bit paradoxical, in view of the present controversies, indecisions and weaknesses of this Church. But that lack of eagerness to recognize its dialectical character may only be the result of the fact that this Church has not yet effectively become conscious of being a fully dialectical Church. Up to the present, we may say, the Church of England has too often been content with a more or less tolerant co-existence, a mere juxta-position of different ideas, points of view, theologies, and practices, having no higher ambition than to keep a kind of precarious peace or rather truce, by letting sleeping dogs lie. But, to that extent, this so-called 'comprehensive' Church of England has failed to rise to the height of its historic and providential vocation. Our Church must bestir itself and *become* a genuine dialectical Church, if it is to do the work for which its position in Western Christendom and its character have marked it out.

A Church which truly deserves to be called 'dialectical,' which accepts and welcomes that character, is further bound to adopt a somewhat peculiar attitude towards itself. The Church of England cannot, of course, identify itself unreservedly with any of the contending theological systems and opinions, either Anglo-Catholic or Evangelical, or Liberal, which it holds in its bosom. On the contrary, a dialectical Church is committed to the view that all these views or particular theologies must *all* be transcended in a higher *synthesis*. And this means the dialectical Church itself must also be transcended, in the sense that its present character, shaped by its internal and never ceasing dialectic, must undergo a progressive change, as the dialectic moves towards a solution.

'A dialectical Church cannot claim for its present views and ways more than a limited and provisional authority. Like all organized societies, it must of course demand of its members a certain minimum loyalty to itself, but it is bound to interpret the word "loyalty" in a peculiar and flexible sense. It cannot without qualification demand of its members loyalty to itself as it now is. It must demand of them loyalty to the terms of the "compromise," which makes possible their co-existence and their growing dialectic. But, this being granted, the truly "loyal" member of the Church will be precisely the one who is striving to see beyond the present state of his Church to something richer and truer.' [16]

Such a dialectical Church appeals from itself, as at present shaped, to itself, as better shaped in the future. Such a Church must be constantly consulting, and closely examining, those sources, from which that better shape and better information may be expected to come. The official formularies of the Church of England, and its tradition of theological method are quite in agreement with this demand. As a matter of fact, the appeal to the Scripture and the appeal to the Church Fathers both leave room for reinterpretation and adjustment, as the Bible and the Fathers come to be better understood.

May I now summarize the third part of this essay about *Anglican synthesis?* Roman Catholicism and Protestantism, as contending systems, represent incompatible theologies, in which truth is mingled with error. On the contrary, the Catholic principle of fulness or comprehensiveness, and the Protestant principle of purity, or rather of a vivid sense of priorities, can and must find their place together in a healthy and balanced Christianity, and especially in a new and deep Anglican dogmatic and theological *synthesis*. This vital and integrated *synthesis* is only a synthesis of what is true, positive and valuable in Roman Catholicism, and of what is true, positive and valuable in Protestantism, and of other elements of truth which both have almost forgotten and are still kept alive in the Orthodox Church. It is by means of a genuine dialectical and multilateral debate that Anglican theologians will be able to determine the conditions and the divers ingredients of this higher Anglican *synthesis*. In my opinion, the fulness of the doctrine and life of the Church of England, and of the Anglican Communion at large, will be utterly Catholic (the Catholicism being taken at its best), and uncompromisingly Protestant or Evangelical (the Protestantism being taken also at its best), and that in a vital and articulated *synthesis*. In this dialectical process, the first stage is to set aside from the conflicting theological systems what is false and out of proportion. The second one will be to keep firmly what is true, positive and healthy in these conflicting systems and ways of life. Finally, the third stage will be to construct again a newly elaborated pattern of theological thought (I wish to avoid the term system) in its proper context, which is that of a living and rediscovered Orthodox faith, keeping in all things the due proportion of the Christian faith.

That dialectical process will mean, no doubt, the death of much which has become habitual, and endeared itself to Anglicans by long familiarity; it will also mean an awakening into a new and fuller life.

As a practical conclusion of this essay, I should like to express, with full sincerity and candour, what seems to me the logical and the truly Christian line of behaviour which ought to be adopted by the priests and the leading laymen of our Church of England, this pre-eminently dialectical Church of Western Christendom.

We must become more and more 'intolerant' of the bigoted

L

and sectarian Catholic who is not an Evangelical, and of the bigoted and sectarian Evangelical who is not a Catholic. Such party men do not really illustrate either the breadth or the depth of the *Anglican synthesis*. On the other hand, the so-called 'moderate' Anglican, who is neither Catholic nor Evangelical, but prefers to follow a kind of practical middle way, which, for our souls' health, ought to be vigorously excluded, is even further from the Anglican vision. The 'no-party party' is indeed the worst of all the parties. For this 'no-party party,' the Church is neither Catholic nor Evangelical, but a lukewarm and complacent mediocrity, which combines a few of the characteristics of both, but misses the fulness of each. In empirical and practical terms, the hope of Anglicanism, or, more concretely, of the Anglican Communion, lies in the loving collaboration, mutual trust and friendship of the out-and-out Evangelicals, and of the out-and-out Anglo-Catholics, but not in some kind of future triumph of a sleepy and self-complacent central churchmanship.

May I end this essay with two biblical quotations? The first is: *He who has an ear, let him hear what the Spirit says to the Churches* (Rev. 2 : 7).

The second quotation gives us this message of the Spirit, in the very words of John the Apostle: *For the message you have heard from the beginning is this: that we should love one another.* [. . .] *My children, love must not be a matter of words or talk; it must be genuine, and show itself in action* (1 John 3 : 11 and 18, N.E.B.).

NOTES

[1] J. V. Langmead Casserley, op. cit., pp. 126–7.

[2] For the second and third parts of this essay, the present writer acknowledges that he owes a large debt of gratitude to Professor H. A. Hodges, Professor of Philosophy in the University of Reading, and especially to his small but golden booklet, *Anglicanism and Orthodoxy: a Study in Dialectical Churchmanship* (S.C.M. Press, 1957). The greater part of the ideas or views expounded in the rest of this essay are not mine, but Professor Hodges's. I shall carefully note the textual quotations, but all the following pages are deeply influenced by this pamphlet, especially by chapter II, 'The Meaning of Anglican Unity,' pp. 26–41.

May I add that I have inserted many personal qualifications and nuances, and that the third part of this essay is more original than the second?

[3] H. A. Hodges, op. cit., p. 27.

[4] Twice the English Prayer Book of 1928 was approved by large majorities in the Convocations of Canterbury and York, and finally in the Church Assembly.

[5] H. A. Hodges, op. cit., p. 30.

[6] H. A. Hodges, op. cit., p. 31.

[7] H. A. Hodges, op. cit., pp. 34-5 (with some small alterations).

[8] On Nov. 4, 1962, Dr. A. R. Vidler, Dean of King's College, Cambridge, made certain criticisms of church services and attitudes of mind in a programme on BBC Television. The debate which followed in the Church Press and elsewhere was rather intemperate and sometimes inaccurate. Dr. Vidler's views can be found in his contribution to *Soundings* (C.U.P., 1962, pp. 239-63). Mr. Paul Ferris has written *The Church of England* (Penguin, 1964)—EDITOR.

[9] H. A. Hodges, op. cit., p. 36.

[10] H. A. Hodges, op. cit., p. 37.

[11] H. A. Hodges, op. cit., pp. 37-8.

[12] The reader may be referred to what I wrote in my book, *Rome and Canterbury: a Biblical and Free Catholicism* (H. Jenkins, 1962), on pp. 210-220 ('restrictions upon the legitimate freedom of a Christian in the sphere of intellectual life'). These pages contain a detailed analysis, enlivened with many quotations, of the famous (or notorious) encyclical *Humani Generis*, which Pius XII promulgated less than three months before his dogmatic definition of the bodily Assumption in heaven of the Blessed Virgin Mary.

[13] H. A. Hodges, op. cit., p. 39 (with some minor alterations).

[14] cf. H. A. Hodges, op. cit., pp. 39 and 47.

[15] cf. H. A. Hodges, op. cit., pp. 40-1.

[16] H. A. Hodges, op. cit., p. 41.

SHORT BIBLIOGRAPHY

G. W. O. Addleshaw, *The High Church Tradition,* 204 pp., Faber, 1941

A. M. Allchin, *The Spirit and the Word,* 95 pp., Faith Press, 1963

J. von Allmen, *Prophétisme Sacramentel,* 311 pp., Delachaux et Niestlé, 1964

E. J. Bicknell (rev. by H. J. Carpenter), *The Thirty-Nine Articles,* 463 pp., Longmans, 1955

Louis Bouyer, *The Spirit and Forms of Protestantism,* 234 pp., Harvill, 1956

Catholicity, a Report by a group of Catholic Anglicans, 56 pp., Dacre Press, 1947

J. Carpenter, *Gore, A Study in Liberal Catholic Thought,* 307 pp., Faith Press, 1960

A. O. J. Cockshut, *Anglican Attitudes,* 128 pp., Collins, 1959

The Fulness of Christ: a Report by a group of Evangelicals, 89 pp., S.P.C.K., 1950

H. Küng, K. Barth and O. Cullman, *Christianity Divided,* 335 pp., Sheed & Ward, 1961

F. J. Leenhardt, *Two Biblical Faiths,* 120 pp., Lutterworth, 1964

J.-L. Leuba, *The New Testament Pattern,* 163 pp., Lutterworth, 1953

H. R. McAdoo, *The Spirit of Anglicanism,* 418 pp., Black, 1965

S. H. Miller and G. E. Wright (Edd.), *Ecumenical Dialogue at Harvard,* 385 pp., Harvard Univ. Press, 1964

P. E. More and F. L. Cross (Edd.), *Anglicanism,* 811 pp., S.P.C.K., 1935

J. K. Mozley, *Some Tendencies in British Theology,* 166 pp., S.P.C.K., 1951

G. F. Nuttall and O. Chadwick, *From Uniformity to Unity, 1662–1962,* 423 pp. S.P.C.K., 1962

D. Paton (Ed.), *Essays in Anglican Self-Criticism,* 238 pp., S.C.M., 1958

J. Pelikan, *The Riddle of Roman Catholicism,* 255 pp., Hodder, 1960

A. M. Ramsey, *F. D. Maurice and the Conflicts of Modern Theology,* 118 pp., C.U.P., 1951

A. M. Ramsey, *From Gore to Temple,* 192 pp., Longmans, 1960

J. A. T. Robinson, *On Being the Church in the World,* 158 pp., S.C.M., 1960

A. M. Stibbs, *God's Church,* 118 pp., I.V.F. 1959

A. M. Stibbs, *Sacrament, Sacrifice and Eucharist,* 93 pp., Tyndale, 1961

G. H. Tavard, *The Quest for Catholicity,* 227 pp., Burns & Oates, 1963

W. H. Griffith Thomas, *The Principles of Theology,* 540 pp., C.B.R.P., 1930

A. R. Vidler, *Essays in Liberality,* 189 pp., S.C.M., 1957

A. R. Vidler (Ed.), *Soundings,* 268 pp., C.U.P., 1962

D. Voll, *Catholic Evangelicalism,* 150 pp., Faith Press, 1963

INDEX